IT'S NOT ALL FLOWERS AND SAUSAGES

MY ADVENTURES IN SECOND GRADE

BY MRS.

D1004665

AS CREATED BY JENN̶

Published by Kaplan Publishing, a division of Kaplan, Inc.
1 Liberty Plaza, 24th Floor
New York, NY 10006

Library of Congress Cataloging-in-Publication Data

Scoggin, Jennifer.
  It's not all flowers and sausages : my adventures in second grade / Jennifer Scoggin As Mrs. Mimi.
    p. cm.
  ISBN 978-1-60714-066-5
  1. Schools--Humor. 2. Teaching--Humor.
  3. School children--Humor. I. Title.
  PN6231.S3S855 2009
  372.1102'07--dc22

                                    2009017494

Printed in the United States of America

10 9 8 7 6 5 4 3 2

ISBN: 978-1-60714-066-5

Kaplan Publishing books are available at special quantity discounts to use for sales promotions, employee premiums, or educational purposes. Please email our Special Sales Department to order or for more information at kaplanpublishing@kaplan.com, or write to Kaplan Publishing, 1 Liberty Plaza, 24th Floor, New York, NY 10006

This book is for my Super Colleagues.
(You know who you are, you fabulous ladies!)
Without you, I would be alone and crying in my supply closet.
I have been lucky to work with and learn from each of you.

And to the Super-est of Super Teachers,
the best teacher I have ever had,
my mom, JoAnne
Thank you.

Contents

Introduction

M Y NAME IS Mrs. Mimi and I am a second-grade teacher in Harlem.

"Hi, Mrs. Mimi!"

When I tell people what I do for a living, I usually get one of three reactions.

Reaction #1: "Oooooo…little kids are sooooo cuuuuuute! I am so jealous! It must be so fun to color and sing all day."

This reaction tends to send me into a bit of a rage, compelling me to regale these individuals with an insanely long laundry list of roles that teachers must balance. I feel the need to inform them of the incredible amount of planning and thought that goes into our days and point out that, unlike those who work in an office, I must complete all my daily tasks while simultaneously holding my own pee for eight hours at a time. *Eight hours!*

Reaction #2: "If I could spend some time volunteering, I would definitely work with children like you do."

Ummmm, moron, teachers get *paid* because we work *insanely hard*. But that's cool, I know you're really online shopping all day in your air-conditioned cubicle and are just feeling incredibly unfulfilled and worthless. Just try not to take it out on teachers next time, okay?

Reaction #3: "Wow! You work there?! You're totally like Michelle Pfeiffer in *Dangerous Minds*!"

Okay. No…just no.

I won't even respond to those who immediately point out that it must be nice to have my summers off. I feel as if they should just be shot.

(Note: Before continuing to read, please begin humming a song you think of as fairly badass. I find that having my own soundtrack helps make me feel even more fabulous than I already am. I mean, don't all inner-city public school teachers have their own soundtrack that follows them around? And wear lots of leather? Yes? No?)

Okay. So now that we've gotten *that* out of the way…

If I could, I would scream, "I am a teacher!" proudly from the highest mountain, but high heels do not lend themselves to intense hikes. Nor do I lend *myself* to anything quite so outdoorsy. Plus, screaming from a mountaintop just seems so cliché. And when you're a teacher, let's face it, there's practically a jungle of clichés for you to fight through, hence the ridiculous reactions I receive from those outside of the world of education when I tell them about my choice of career. Like I said, I don't do outside and I certainly don't do cliché. Let's take a look at some of these awfully inaccurate teacher clichés and poke some holes in them, shall we? Because I don't see myself represented anywhere...

Well, first we have the stereotypical image of an elementary school teacher who loves terrible thematic sweaters, sensible shoes, and necklaces made exclusively from dried pasta products and Tempra paint. This teacher may also be sporting some sort of dangly thematic earring that may or may not blink. Perhaps she is brandishing a pointer as well. I think this teacher's soundtrack might include hits from artists such as Raffi. Fortunately, she exists mainly in the cloudy, and very delusional, childhood memories of the classroom held by many who seem to think they went to school in a Norman Rockwell painting or something. I resent this teacher on many levels. But perhaps what I find most insulting is she is portrayed as a smiling idiot who is completely void of any sort of sass. She's just so…well, I think the macaroni necklace says it all.

I teach elementary school and somehow manage to dress myself every day without resorting to anything that can be purchased at the grocery store. In all honesty, I think of myself (and my school wardrobe) as pretty fabulous. And while I may not have a lithium-induced smile plastered on my face and Raffi blasting from my room, I do love my little friends. A lot. So much so, that I have a hard time leaving school at school and often hear myself continuing to talk about the adventures in my classroom long after my friends go home at 3. And, if I'm not talking *about* my students, I'm talking to other adults as if *they were* my students. Like at home with my husband, Mr. Mimi, I might find myself saying something like, "Honey, is that really where you want to leave your shoes? Do we want this to be a place where people have to worry about tripping over shoes left all over?" Yeah, I think it's safe to say Mr. Mimi loves (read: tolerates) this little habit of mine. I've tried to reform, but there's something about spending the entire day with 20 small people who quickly become more like a little family that makes it hard to leave it all behind in the classroom. I have never thought of teaching as just a job.

Okay. For our next cliché, we have the kind of teacher made popular by many a sitcom. This teacher appears to have insane amounts of free time during the school day. She spends the majority of this free time hanging out in the mahogany-furnished teachers' lounge. This lounge is usually also equipped with stainless steel appliances and could not be a further cry from the sad, mouse-poo–encrusted little microwave shoved in the corner of one of my colleague's classrooms. (Yeah, my colleague drew the short straw.) This teacher, who is usually wearing a very low-cut and entirely dry-clean-only outfit, can be seen furrowing her brow with concern at a passing student approximately a nanosecond before she begins flirting with the abundance of hot male teachers at her school. Her soundtrack would have a variety of Top 40 hits such as "Sexy Back" and "Promiscuous Girl." Again, she seems to have nowhere else to be. Yet somehow, back in reality, I never have any free time and spend most of my precious minutes alone running around the classroom, you know, doing stuff for the children? But hey, I guess we all have our priorities.

Let me be clear about something here. I never have a free minute between the hours of 8 and 3. Never. Ever. Having the time to pee feels like a luxury most days.

And finally, we have the overly done stereotype of the urban schoolteacher who is clad in extremely form-fitting leather. Her soundtrack is comprised of exclusively gangsta rap with the exception of that one heart-wrenching song of triumph. This song is reserved for the precise moment in which she successfully reaches every child and turns each of their lives around. This teacher can be imagined braving the harsh city streets armed with only a pen and her own smug determination. Although I think she is intended to inspire, she typically sends me into spastic fits of anger. I mean, first of all, leather is totally not practical for an environment in which there is no control over the thermostat. I mean, the average year-round temperature of my classroom is a balmy 86 degrees. And second of all, you're setting the rest of us up to fail, sister friend! I mean, *every* child is a success story? Those are dangerous stats...hero-complex much?

Like I said earlier, I teach in Harlem and am proud to say that I have never worn leather anywhere but on my feet. I am also proud to say that I have been fairly successful during my time there. However, I will never say that I have reached every child. In fact, on many an occasion, I know that I have failed them. Sometimes they are small failures, like when I dodge a conversation about farts by telling students to "just go get a drink of water and sit back down." And sometimes they are larger failures, like when I just can't find a way to help a child to make a year's worth of progress in reading. That's honest. But that is just a part of teaching, a very real part that my leather-wearing friend seems to have completely bypassed or conveniently ignored.

I guess all of these clichés have their place. I can even find them somewhat entertaining once I get past all of the aspects of these women that are blatantly offensive and mock my profession. What really bothers me the most about all these clichés is that I don't see myself in any of these images. Where is all the petty drama over photocopies and bullshit meetings? Where is the administrative ridiculousness? And where is all the urine?

This book is part of my story of teaching. By no means is it the whole story. I'm not sure that would fit into one book, what with my flair for dramatic storytelling and the complexity that is the American public school classroom. Plus, I'm not done teaching, don't have all the answers, and definitely have a lot more to learn. So this is part of my story, for now. It grows out of my blog, the purpose of which was to give me an anonymous space to vent my frustrations and possibly give voice to some of the ridiculous hurdles to good teaching. I had to make it funny, or else I would be forced to scream into my pillow each and every night. Yet please keep in mind that this is a *story,* not a transcription, of my experiences in the classroom. Names have been changed, characters have been collapsed, stories have been dramatized, and liberties have been taken. For real.

Let's not get it twisted. This book is not an attack on the places I have worked, nor is it aimed at the people with whom I have worked. You see, I don't work in a "bad school." At all. In fact, I work in a very good school, a school that has made a tremendous amount of progress and is making a truly positive difference in the lives of children. Seriously. *That* is what I think is so frustrating. I work in a "good school" with many hardworking people who are committed to change, yet the shenanigans you'll read about are still happening and interfering with progress.

This is a story (an hilarious story…if you ask me) of my life in the classroom and, ironically, how my little friends are often the people who save me when I think I'm drowning in a sea of administrative, organizational, and bureaucratic bullshit.

Holy Crap, It's August!

SOMEHOW, WHEN MY childhood self would imagine my destined-to-be-fabulous future self, the picture never involved quite so much...urine.

I mean so much of my daily work life involves pee...all kinds of pee. Let's see, every day, I decide when and how often 20 little people get to pee. I also regularly clean up mouse pee. I live in fear of the dreaded bathroom accident, which then necessitates dealing with puddles of pee. Each morning, as I make my way down the hall to my classroom, I am greeted by the faint odor of pee that wafts out of the boys' bathroom. And finally, I hold my own pee for hours at a time, which I believe has led to this odd obsession with pee.

1

I am a teacher, and I'm living the dream.

Yes, my childhood self neglected to imagine all the pee. I guess I was too busy picturing myself as a famous actress. Real original, right? But I have always loved acting. I starred in play after play in high school and thought I was pretty hot stuff. It seemed inevitable, to me at least, that my future would be filled with thunderous applause and flashing lights. And honestly, my predictions weren't that far off, if you substitute the thunderous applause after my stunning performance with children clapping and laughing through my multidimensional reading of *Charlie and the Chocolate Factory* complete with voices for each character. (I do a mean read aloud. Seriously, you should hear my Violet Beauregarde.) And as for the flashing lights…well, I always have fire drills.

Perhaps I should have seen the writing on the wall, because my life has always revolved around schools and been filled with teachers. My mother is a teacher, so I grew up surrounded by mounds of papers to be corrected and was put to work decorating bulletin boards as soon as I was old enough to wield a stapler. Every August, my mother, grandmother, and I would brave the heat, pack up our little orange cooler, and head off to school. As soon as we walked in the door, I felt overwhelmed with the stench of learning. You know what I mean: that smell of glue, construction paper, industrial cleaner, and freshly sharpened pencils. To this day, I still find that smell addictive and it always brings me back to those summer days when we set up my mother's classroom.

In preparation for my Bulletin Board Extravaganza (I took my childhood job very seriously), I would treat myself to a trip to the school's supply room, where a literal rainbow of construction paper and endless bottles of Tempra paint surrounded me. As a huge nerd and an only child who spent days working tirelessly on her own art projects, it was like a utopia. I spent hours color coordinating and stylizing her bulletin boards. And when I was done with her room, I walked up and down the halls and pimped my services out to her colleagues. Because they were all there. During the summer. When most of you thought they had their feet up and their faces down in a drink.

Fast-forward 20 years and I'm getting ready to start my seventh year of teaching in a public elementary school in Harlem. My summer is officially over. As always, my summer To Do list is several pages long and includes scintillating items such as "clean out closet" (the pressures of the school year always seem to trump any sort of project that might improve one's personal life) and "read entire Horrible Harry series." (You should see some of the looks I get on public transportation when I whip out 48 pages of emergent reading. It's usually a mixed bag of "Oh, poor thing…but good for you for tackling literacy at age thirty!" and "What an idiot!"). Don't get me wrong…it's pretty rad to get summers off, but don't let that term "summer" fool you. It is not an entire season in which I cease working. Rather it is seven weeks of time, which just happen to occur in the summer months, during which I re-write old curriculum, read hundreds of children's chapter books, and scour stores for deals on school supplies. Although, if I'm honest with myself, I should start adding summer To Dos such as "drinking fruity cocktails" or "catching up on morning TV" to the list. Hey, I'm not Superwoman.

I like to think about the month of July as one long Saturday. Your workweek is over, and Saturday is filled with so many possibilities. (Granted, in the teacher's world, Saturday's possibilities usually include activities such as catching up on sleep, correcting papers, and/or writing lesson plans, but still, you get to do it at home with a glass of something with an umbrella in it.) Then there is also the comforting knowledge that you have another day left to get everything done before the week begins again. But Sunday always comes and you know that feeling that you get on Sunday nights? Where you had a good weekend, but are kind of bummed that it's over and a little bit anxious about all the errands you didn't do? Well, for teachers, August is always like one big, long Sunday.

I was deep into my summer haze when I heard the tinkling sound of a text message.

I checked my phone and found a message from my colleague informing me that she had just picked up the new Barnes and Noble planner and had mapped out her whole first week.

She can't be serious.

I immediately went running down the stairs, grabbed car keys, threw on my new fabulous grassy green peep-toe flats, and jumped in the car. I'm off to Barnsey! (That's my pet name for Barnes and Noble...although Mr. Mimi refers to it as that place where I deposit all our money, but really? I could be doing worse things with my/our/his money. It could be crack or something.)

I enter the store and am immediately distracted by all the shiny new hardcovers. You see, with some time off, I've actually (drumroll, please) had time to read for pleasure! As I start to peruse the buy-two-get-the-third-free table I wonder, "What am I doing here again? I could swear I came in for something specific."

Oh!

Work!

Starts next week!

Planner! That's right, I'm here for a planner. Yes, buying that planner will get me in the right frame of mind. I'm sure that within moments of purchasing it, I'll go home and plan brilliant new units, think of engaging new author studies...you name it! I'm psyching myself up while simultaneously congratulating myself on my teaching prowess when I realize that I can't find the flippin' planner anywhere! I've been to the "Teacher Reference" section and the "Education" section. Nothing.

Maybe it's a sign that I can't find the planner. Yes! *A sign!* The universe is sending me a sign. I should *definitely* leave teaching and go work at Papyrus...I'd have such great stationary and no pressure. Or, perhaps it is finally time to pursue my dream job of naming nail polish colors...

I stop and debate.

Let's see...I do feel pretty beat down after last year. I mean, at the end it felt like we were practically wading around in mounds of our own bullshit. There were so many times I wondered if the people around me were doing everything in their power to make teaching harder than it needs to be...all the screwed up copy orders, phone calls in the middle of a lesson, botched field trips, endless paperwork, and people who refuse to parent their child. (Yes, I am aware that I have just used "parent" as a verb, but I am from Connecticut and we frequently use "summer" as a verb as well. It's not our fault per se; it's just the way of our people.)

But...I do like my job. Most of the time. I love the time I spend with the kids at least. Some of the other adults I work with? Well, we'll get into that later, but I'm not ready to leave the kids. Honestly, I can't imagine spending the last seven years anywhere else. With all my bitching and moaning, what do I love about it? (Prepare yourself...cue the sappy, inspirational music à la Lifetime Movie of the Week, please.) I love shaking my students' little hands every morning. I love that feeling I get when I'm in the middle of a really fabulous lesson and everything just seems to come together. I love how exciting it is to plan a new unit of study with my Super Colleagues. At this point, I can't imagine spending the day with adults anymore—my friends are just way cooler. Oh, and Sharpies, I love all the Sharpies. And getting to write on the board, of course.

Sick, right?

Perhaps it's been all those years of inhaling chalk dust (which transitioned into years of huffing dry-erase marker), and reveling in my ability to stop small children with a single raise of the eyebrow...but I know I'm not ready to move on yet.

I begin to wander around the children's section hoping to reignite my beginning-of-the-year flame with a fabulous new read aloud, but all of my bravado is gone. I'm crushed. What kind of teacher am I anyway if I can't even *find* the planner??

And then, as I turned the corner, the seas parted. There it was. My new planner. And in *three colors*! There's never been a choice before! I can have it in purple or green or blue—the possibilities feel endless. Life is good again. That's it: I'll go back to work. Sorry Papyrus, your loss. I'm back!

And for those of you who are thinking, "Oh, poor teacher, you have to go back to work after three months off," I have several things to say to you. One, shut up. Two, it is not three months: in reality it is more like seven weeks. But we've already covered this…try to keep up, okay? Three, I'm sure we could list off little perks to your job, too, or do you not want to admit to your bonus check, cushy office chair, and expense account right now? I didn't think so. Shall I keep going?

THERE ARE OFFICIALLY five workdays before the kids come back, which really isn't a lot of time when you factor in all the welcome-back chatting. Teachers are notoriously superchatty. We love nothing more than to interrupt one another mid-bulletin board, or to linger in a doorway making small talk. As much as I want to scream and shove the Lingering Chatterer out of my doorway, I have also been guilty of this little habit myself...something about denying the mountain of work you know is waiting for you in your room and fooling yourself that you are having a necessary dialogue about a student (that just happens to include a discussion of last night's episode of *Grey's Anatomy*).

However, this year, the administration decided to start out the year with a retreat, instead of time working in our classrooms. In a sense, it's almost like Officially Sanctioned Chatting since we will all be corralled into the same space for two days and unable to work on our classrooms, but I doubt that is what the administration had in mind.

Evidently our principal, who we will call The Visionary, thinks that this retreat, which is to be held in a very fancy-pants conference center, will make us "feel more like professionals." This line of thinking interestingly assumes that prior to setting foot in the fancy-pants conference center I felt like a nonprofessional loser or even a faux-professional, but I digress. Attendance was voluntary, but really...who wants to be the jerk who doesn't show up to the first ever retreat? Plus, even though I have occasionally had the desire to throw my hot coffee at him, I do think The Visionary is brilliant. He has truly turned around our school and made it a much more positive place for children (despite all my bitching and moaning.) For real! So I gave him and this whole retreat idea the benefit of the doubt.

I reluctantly set my alarm clock for the first time in seven weeks and laid out my clothes for the next day. Great care is always taken at this time of year to choose an outfit that says, "I'm still in summer mode, but I guess I'll go to work." I, of course, would also like to try to look put together for as long as possible, because I know by mid-October I will be my usual disheveled, paint and snot (theirs not mine) covered self. As much as I hate to admit it, I went to sleep nerdily excited about all the great things I fooled myself into thinking would come from this conference. More authentic assessments! Better integrated units of study! More engaging student projects! I finally drifted off to sleep with the idea of two uninterrupted days of planning and working with my Super Colleagues dancing in my head.

As I walked into the conference center the next morning, I was handed a new canvas tote with the school's name and mascot stitched on the side. The tote contained a notepad, keychain, and pen. Sadly, I think we all thought the free stuff was pretty sweet, but most teachers have a bit of a scavengeresque, pack-rattish side to them. I mean, many of us also save toilet paper tubes, egg crates, and old tuna fish cans, so free pens seemed fairly hot.

Anyhow, the retreat started off with a lot of fanfare, and not much else in the way of actual work. None of us really knew what to expect from this retreat. However, all the Teacher Swag left us feeling as if it could be fairly promising. I glanced at our agendas for the day. Much like my awkward teenage camp experiences, this retreat was going to be all about building trust and respect. And the first item of the day was karma. Yes, you read correctly, karma.

The Weave was the first administrator to speak. She is my vice principal and direct supervisor, who I have alternatively loved and hated over the last seven years. (I'm fairly certain she would say the same thing about me, too.) Sometimes she is your best ally and at other times, she is clearly over the drama and could give a shit. She is famous for scheduling field trips on a Sunday and then getting pissed at *us* when someone points out her mistake. She is a pro at ignoring pressing issues, making it clear that often times, despite her title and job description, she does not want to deal. Period. On those days, you can almost certainly find her reading the newspaper in the cafeteria while parents drop off their children and teachers pick up their classes around her. If she's not there, you might find her in her office…reading the paper. Evidently she likes to be up on her current events. Unfortunately, sometimes the most pressing current events include the shit going down all around her.

Now, I am not being completely fair here (imagine that). At times, The Weave is amazing. Last year, I had a particularly difficult month and found myself crying in her office after school wondering if I should just quit. (I know, odd choice of confidant, right?) But she listened and talked me out of quitting. She really talked me in from the ledge.

So, on this first day of the retreat, The Weave managed to put aside her morning paper and began by discussing her own career in the classroom. She discussed her uncanny ability to use humor to alleviate the stress of teaching. After her sagelike advice to "just laugh it off," she transitioned into her talk about karma. She advised us to make sure that the "karma" in our classroom encourages student learning and exploration. Apparently, she went Zen on us over the summer.

Oh, and as you attempt to find *your* Zen and imagine this scene, make sure that you include The Weave's navel-baring shirt. Distracted from your Zen yet? Yes…my vice principal was wearing a navel-baring shirt. Okay, maybe it wasn't *created* to be navel baring but it certainly bared way too much navel today. The professionalism is just overwhelming, especially as we sit in the fancy-pants conference center for "real professionals."

I won't bother to transcribe her words of wisdom in their entirety here because I'm really hoping that you will stick with me and read the remainder of this book; however, I am including a few of the highlights from her inspirational talk. (Secretly, I have always wanted to be one of those commentators on ESPN during sporting events, not because I have a wealth of knowledge about sports, but because I tend to be opinionated and find myself to be hilarious. Who wouldn't want to hear what I think about the yellow team's tight little pants? So consider this my first stab at commentating from the sidelines.)

Highlight #1

"We have the most smartest staff I've ever worked with. You should be confident in how smart you are."

And we have a fumble! Man down on the field! Um, yea, thanks for your vote of confidence in our intellectual abilities, but you should really practice sentences in your head first...

Highlight #2

"Make sure that your classroom is relaxed, children can move about freely to get supplies, and that the room is buzz-

ing with discussion. *But, don't forget…we value task on time, quiet children, and sticking to the schedule.*"

Um, what? I'm fairly certain that your last two sentences cancel each other out, sister. Although, oddly enough, this type of contradiction is not at odds with many of the demands that are placed upon teachers during the school year. Frequently we are told that our opinions are valid and welcome, and, well, we all know that *that* isn't true.… I mean the terms "teachers' opinions" and "valid and welcome" are diametrically opposed, right?

Maybe her words are an enigma wrapped in a conundrum and I'm just not smart enough to understand her ruminations on karma even though, yes, I am one of the "most smartest."

I contemplated The Weave's advice (and clear lack of mastery of the English language) for the rest of our morning session. And then…cue the semi-stale wraps please…it was time for lunch.

At our school, the humble employees fall into one of two categories. The first category contains my Super Colleagues (and myself, duh) who rock endlessly in our classrooms. The *other* category is comprised of those who have no observable work ethic. These teachers (read: wastes of space) refuse to do anything that is not spelled out in their mythical contract and appear to exist solely to make our lives more difficult. You don't have to be a teacher to know what I'm talking about. You can picture that sack of hair in your office that does absolutely nothing, makes no effort, and somehow still has a job. Just take a moment...got them in your head? Mmmmm, me too. Kind of makes you want to poke yourself in the eye, doesn't it?

Today I became reacquainted with one of the most offensive offenders who regularly makes me want to scream into my pillow at night.

(Drumroll, please) Let me introduce The Fanny Pack. The Fanny Pack and I are forced to "work" together on a fairly regular basis at school. I put "work" in quotations because allegedly she is supposed to work with children who speak English as a Second Language. However, after interacting with her for the last three years, I am not convinced that she is aware of this crucial part of her job description. She is one of the infamous "out of the classroom" teachers who evidently takes "out of the classroom" to mean that she no longer has any responsibility to children or has to even attempt to act like she's working. And I'm sorry to all of you out-of-the-classroom teachers who rock it out every day, but, honestly, this woman is sullying your good name. So blame her, not me.

To begin with, The Fanny Pack always has this very confused expression on her face, like she's not quite sure

15

what she's doing in a school building. She frequently wanders around the building in search of the students with whom she is supposed to be working. I have no idea why she finds them so difficult to find...I mean, it's not like we rotate classrooms. We are in the same freaking place every day, woman! And then, we have the fanny pack. *Fanny pack?* Yes, I said fanny pack. And not an I'm-trying-to-make-a-functional-fashion-statement fanny pack. A hideous, primary colored, nylon fanny pack with the oh-so-sexy black plastic clippy thing. Need I say more?

I first noticed this waste of budget dollars, I'm sorry, I meant "colleague," as she rapidly approached the line for lunch. We were all involved in our own conversations about summer, but frankly, it was hard not to see her coming and even harder not to stare. You see, over the summer she had evidently spent her time selecting a brand-new fanny pack. It was made of a lovely shiny synthetic material in a jubilant shade of red. It screamed, "Look at me! I have no idea how to do my job!" Really, I felt as if the red was a little much, it was almost taunting me, and I thought to myself, "Self, this is the year that you will sneak a peek inside that fanny pack."

But my daydreams of what might possibly be in said fanny pack (A snack? Dental floss? Condoms? Her meds?) were cruelly interrupted when The Fanny Pack *shoved* me into several of our other colleagues as she cut in the line for lunch. Wait, let me say that again. *She cut in the line for lunch!* On the first day back, when we're all supposed to at least pretend to play nicely in the sandbox together.

And, I'm sorry, but aren't we all adults? Who tries to get cuts anymore? We watched her push her way up to the table, refuse to make eye contact with anyone, and then proceed to shove several rolls and a handful of mustard packets into her new school tote. The whole thing really just warmed my heart…I mean, way to dive right back into it and put some good karma out there right from the start!

But this year is a new year. So in an effort to usher in a more positive attitude, I promise that today will be a new day. And today, I will not judge.

Now tomorrow, that's another story…

THE RETREAT IS OVER in two days, and it is fairly obvious to everyone that we have just supremely wasted two days. In fact, despite our administration's best efforts to get off on the right foot, it was more of a mad dash to the starting line…like we were all caught with our pants down or something. Metaphorical pants of course (this isn't *that* kind of book).

We had been promised hour after uninterrupted hour of planning time with our grade level teams, however, when all was said and done, I think we might have only done 30 minutes of actual work. The rest of the time we spent listening to lectures on karma, doing trust falls, and other various icebreakers.

I decided to shake off the oh-so-ironic bad karma of our retreat, and dive into getting my classroom ready. While I may not be a fan of trust falls, one thing I *do* love about the beginning of the year is getting my room ready and organized. There's something about seeing my classroom all set up before the first day of school. Desks are at perfect right angles, name tags are clean and easy to read, bright paper is on every wall, and there is row after row of perfectly organized books...I think I might be drooling a little. All that organization! The Sharpies, the Post-its, and the To Do lists filled with crossed off tasks...it's like a slice of heaven for me (and for every other giant nerd out there).

At my school, I am an organizational goddess. It may not sound sexy to you, but to me, nothing is hotter than a drawer full of labeled and color-coded files or a spreadsheet with read alouds arranged by genre and cross-referenced by potential purposes.

Keep in mind that I did not start out this way. There is something about teaching that almost forces you to love order and routine. Being disorganized equals having a shitty day. I first learned about this kind of pain in my second year of teaching, when trying to decide how to organize pencils for my students. The memory of my previous year, in which pencils lay strewn about the floor, unsharpened and without a home, literally struck fear in my heart.

Yes, pencils have the ability to drive me insane (and every other teacher if she's honest with herself). You heard me right.

In that previous year, pencils ruined my life. They were on the floor, shoved in desks, and the source of much riotous behavior, yet were somehow never available for any actual writing.

Cries of:

"I don't have a pencil!"

"You stole my pencil…that's mine!"

"My pencil doesn't write!"

"Where's my pencil? It was in my desk."

"Mrs. Mimi! Mrs. Mimi! Pencil! Pencil!"

filled the air.

I tried everything to deal with the Great Pencil Crisis of 2003. I numbered pencils, wrote names on pencils, color-coded pencils to match groups of students, passed out and collected pencils and, in a desperate move, actually Velcroed pencils to the wall so that students had to return their pencil to its assigned spot after each use.

Yeah, I took it that far.

So in my second year of teaching, I decided I was determined to not let pencils take over my brain yet again. I, Mrs. Mimi, was going to conquer pencils once and for all. I mean, that's why I went back to school and got a master's degree, right?

After a long day of setting up my classroom, I headed to Kmart with two of my colleagues to purchase various school supplies, organizational tools, and (insert ominous music here) the dreaded pencils.

I was confident. I was smug. I was ready to take on the pencil and show it who was boss.

Yet as I stood in front of a massive wall of pencils, my confidence wavered. Do I want everyone to share pencils or have their own pencils? Do I number them again? Do I put a bunch of pencils in the middle of the table?

I could feel my heart begin to race. Maybe I hadn't really thought this through. Maybe I would have to sacrifice another year to the Great Pencil Crisis.

I discussed this oh-so-important decision with my colleagues at length. However, rather than calmly coming to a conclusion, we proceeded to bring into question our qualifications for even being teachers and promptly burst into tears.

Yes, we were in tears in the office supply aisle of Kmart. The picture of professionalism, I know.

ME: (sob) "I just can't decide what to do..."

COLLEAGUE #1: (in a trembling voice, every statement actually sounding more like a question) "I think I'm going to go with individual supplies? I mean, is that right? What are you doing? I'm so confused?"

COLLEAGUE #2: (eyes welling up with tears) "I always thought I was a communal supplies person, but now...now... I just don't know."

What happened to my confident, kinda arrogant (hey, I admit it) self? I mean, do I not have advanced degrees in education? Aren't I the one who prides herself on her color-coded, uber-organized To Do lists? Am I not the same girl whose mother pimped her out for her bulletin board–making skills since the time when she was old enough to wield a stapler? And now I can't make a decision about stupid pencils?! It's amazing how these small, essentially minor details can take over and render a teacher totally useless. I have seen many a fabulous teacher break down because she felt like she was drowning in logistics.

After some deep breathing (and a trip to the pub down the street for several beers), I finally went with individual numbered pencils in individual toolboxes. And I never looked back.

THESE DAYS I confidently shop for back-to-school supplies with reckless abandon, which is then followed by intense periods of guilt and rage. Yep, that sounds about right. By reckless abandon, I mean I throw just about anything in my cart…I know what I need and strut up and down the aisles of Staples secure in my eight years of teaching experience. By guilt, I mean those "extras" that I throw in the cart because they are "cute," and "seem like a good idea at the time" when I know deep down that they will spend several months in the bottom of a closet collecting mouse poo. And by rage, I mean the anger I feel as I tally up receipts. I love my kids, but really, why am I buying all this stuff for them?

Yes, back to school shopping can be quite the emotional roller coaster for teachers, full of dramatic twists and turns. (Which comes as no surprise to Mr. Mimi, who thinks I am constantly working to win some sort of trophy for dramatic performance. Untrue. Flattering that he appreciates my love of the theater, but untrue.)

As I enter Staples this year, I am a flurry of energy armed with a color-coded list. I can practically hear McFadden and Whitehead singing "Ain't No Stoppin' Us Now," because I've got the groove. I grab a cart and am off! My first priority, plastic toolboxes on sale for 99¢ each. Which yes, sounds like a good deal, but I do think it is slightly bullshit, because they *used* to go on sale for 25¢ each just a few years ago. Geez. I sound old. (I have also been known to complain about the price of eggs....)

I emerge from behind a giant display of notebooks and...there they are. But wait! There are stacks upon stacks, but there are only two colors—pink and purple. Now, I am all about "you get what you get and you don't get upset" but I am also all about avoiding unnecessary complaining. I mean, I can't stick a little boy I hardly know with a pink toolbox. And don't get all gender-y on me, either! Boys can absolutely choose pink shirts, backpacks, toolboxes, etc. (Mr. Mimi happens to look very sexy in his new pink power tie), but I do *not* believe in forcing the pink upon them. Not because I worry about their disappointment, but because I think I might explode if they even *think* of complaining about something I have provided them at my own expense. Selfless, I know.

I immediately abandon my cart, crestfallen. I am about to leave, when I run into a friendly salesperson (a rare, rare finding at Staples in my experience). There is a glimmer of hope.

ME: "Um, do you happen to have any more of those plastic toolboxes?"

HIM: "There's quite a few right there, miss."

ME: (He called me "miss"! Maybe I'm not so old after all. Insert dazzling smile.) "Yes, but I teach second grade and I can't imagine giving my boys a pink toolbox." (Maintain dazzling smile.)

HIM: "Well, of course. Let's see..."

And he leads me back to another display filled with blue, green, and clear toolboxes! Hooray! I thank the kind man and practically skip back to my abandoned cart. I eagerly count out 22 toolboxes in a variety of colors.

Dismissing the guilt I have felt about overbuying in previous years, I then move onto those wonderful cardboard displays located along the aisles that I have convinced myself are full of fabulous deals. I understand that they are probably not huge deals, but just having them be separate from the other merchandise and stored in a jaunty cardboard bin makes them feel more special.

I begin to toss all kinds of goodies into my cart: Crayola Crayons and markers, bottle after bottle of Elmer's glue, fun erasers, a pencil sharpener, glue sticks, pencils, and dozens and dozens of two-pocket folders.

My cart starts to look like my classroom threw up in it: it is a rainbow-filled vessel brimming with brand-new, shiny school supplies.

My heart is practically bursting. Seriously, I think I may have giggled as I piled twelve new colors of dry-erase markers into my cart.

And I'm done. I wheel myself over to checkout, where another pleasant salesperson (Wow...there are two!) rings me up. I load pile after pile after pile of stuff onto the counter, watching the register tape spew out of the cash register and begin to touch the floor. Really, it did reach the floor.

It was almost like a switch had been flipped. And just like clockwork, here comes the rage.

Why the hell am I spending my money, not to mention my time, on this gloriously sunny day, buying school supplies that should be bought be either *their parents* or *the school*?!

Have I ever told you that I have never, *not once,* been supplied with a pencil? That's right...eight years of teaching and not one damn pencil. The city for which I work spends all kinds of money catering lunches and employing all sorts of people who have never set foot in a classroom yet get to tell me what to do and *no one* has even *thought* that *maybe* they should give the teachers freaking pencils!

But, like I always do, I put on a brave face and hand over my debit card (sigh). I am so all talk.

After spending the next morning hauling all of my bags from the Staples Spending Spree 2008 up to my classroom, I head back down to the office to pick up the supplies that actually do get purchased by the school. Teachers spend hours on supply requests at the end of the year, but somehow this September I receive a handful of rubber bands, some googley eyes, and a bunch of the crappy glue sticks that dry up after two uses. Oh, and I got a listening center. No books on tape, but a listening center. No pencils. No folders. No erasers. We seem to have forgone the basics in pursuit of an obsession with appearances. You see, the bathrooms have been covered in new murals, there are new rugs in the lobby, and fancy new furniture in the main office, but no pencils.

At our staff meeting later that day, our principal, The Visionary, dealt the final blow. He announced that this year, we would not be receiving any paper. None. We are now expected to teach sans paper.

I know, it doesn't make sense to me either.

Does anyone look at a doctor and say, "Hey there, Doctor, just FYI, no bandages this year…not in the budget"? The answer is no. No. No one says that. Because it is ridiculous.

Equally ridiculous is the reasoning behind this decision to withhold paper. Teachers will not be receiving any paper this year because our school is "Going Green."

Now, I love the environment and am all for Going Green, but I think this might be going a bit too far. Not to mention a bit hypocritical. I mean, we separate our paper into a recycling bin in our classrooms, yet everyday the custodial staff just combines our recycling with the regular garbage and puts it all out on the curb together. Oh, and the Styrofoam trays in the cafeteria…are those Green? What about the memos I receive from the office in triplicate that are riddled with typos and unfit to send home? How do they fit into this new environmental initiative?

And so, sadly, I have been driven to steal. It is truly a dark day.

While the administration was busy organizing the Worst Free Lunch Ever (seriously, macaroni salad should *not* resemble a soup because of a horrifying amount of mayonnaise), three of us ducked down to the basement.

It was brilliant. Just like Charlie's Angels…except

dustier. We skanked around abandoned furniture and slinked around ancient textbooks until...

Jackpot! Forgotten boxes of paper. As we filled our arms with the precious booty, we considered spreading the word to our other colleagues, but then...as we remembered dirty looks, hallway snubs, and the general laziness of some...we decided it would be our little secret.

Mmmwwaaaa hahahahahaaaaaa! Suckers.

Maybe I don't feel too bad about the Great Paper Caper after all.

$\mathcal{U}$NFORTUNATELY, A LACK of paper was not the only ridiculous obstacle we faced at the beginning of the year.

(Sigh) I am already exhausted and the kids haven't even come back yet. How many days until kids come back? All this adult time is really getting to me.

I returned to work the next day ready to plan with my Super Colleagues. We had a long list of subjects to tackle and we began by discussing our upcoming unit in science. We are going to start working with soil. According to the standards, the kids need to classify different types of soil, examine what is in the soil, and blah, blah, blah.

We are ready to go…psyched to plan. Pens are out and poised anxiously above the page waiting for genius to issue forth from our lips. And then:

ME: "Uh (yes, I started with "Uh." You know I'm bound to be brilliant when I start with "Uh"), so, do we *have* any soil to use?"

SUPER COLLEAGUE: "Uh (equally brilliant), no."

ME: "Hmmm. Interesting."

SUPER COLLEAGUE: "I guess we could go to the park and dig some up."

ME: "That's sad."

In walks The Weave, vice principal du jour. Awesome. We ask her. Silly us.

ME: "So, is there any soil for us to use in the science lab?"

THE WEAVE: "No."

ME: "Super."

SUPER COLLEAGUE: "We're struggling with how to get through our series of lessons on soil without any, um, soil."

THE WEAVE: "You can work it out."

SUPER COLLEAGUE: "Do you have any ideas for us?"

THE WEAVE: "I'm sure you can find *pictures* of dirt somewhere. Just have them imagine the dirt."

Ah, yes! Why didn't we think of that? Imagine the
dirt, boys and girls. Oh, boys and girls, did you know that
sometimes scientists sit quietly in a room and imagine
the thing they want to study? Then they write down what
they've learned by using their imagination. Science is all
make-believe! We can all really fly! The Tooth Fairy is
real! When a bell rings, an angel gets its wings!

As you can see, the bullshit is so deep that I'm starting to lose my grip on reality. I guess I'm off to the garden
center because I'm pretty sure I didn't see any bags of
potting soil laying around the school's basement on my
last trip.

AND NOW, IT'S TIME for a heartwarming moment
sponsored by the school's main office.
Exhausted by my preparations and anxious for the year
to just get started, I stopped by the main office to put in
a request for copies. Oh, did I forget to mention that the
whole "Going Green" thing only includes the teachers,

and not the remainder of the staff? Evidently, we are the only ones who will be forced to have an environmental conscience this year...everyone else is off the hook. So the support staff in the main office have access to heinous amounts of paper. Foolishly, I thought that our newly found environmental consciousness would extend itself to an all-encompassing spirit of teamwork and caring about one another. Silly me. Unfortunately, many individuals in the main office have taken this opportunity to wield their power in ways that make my job impossible and show no regard for the purpose of our work...you know, to teach kids and all.

I put in a request for 20 copies of homework packets for the first week of school. I specifically asked that the packet be double sided, reducing the amount of paper used for each packet from eight pages down to four. Instead, I received 140 *single-sided* copies, wasting approximately 1,040 pieces of paper. (Yes, I did the math.)

Ah. Very Green. Very Green indeed.

IN A LAST-DITCH EFFORT to try to collect the supplies we were unwilling to beg, borrow, or steal ourselves, my team wrote a letter to parents requesting the donation of certain odds and ends. The list included things such as composition notebooks, erasers, tissues, and pencils. Nothing too fancy or over the top...so we thought.

Letters were mailed out to parents so that they could take advantage of the back-to-school sales that taunt teachers throughout the month of August.

I was overwhelmed by the generosity of many parents. Some parents even purchased everything on our list, which was above and beyond our expectations. Super, right?

Um, yeah.

I was walking down the hall when I heard, "You Mrs. Mimi?"

ME: "Yes. Hi."

HER: "Bitch, listen..."

And then she proceeded to rip me a new one. Evidently she was upset that I requested that each family provide two composition notebooks and a package of pencils. Granted, in no way did I *require* that each family send in those supplies, I merely *requested* some help since I am usually left to buy 90 percent of the class' day-to-day supplies. However, my efforts to assuage her anger were met with much finger waving and it was at this point that I noticed her long, red, shiny acrylic nails.

Now, I hate to admit it, but I myself had acrylic nails all through high school. For those of you who are currently sporting plastic fingernails, I'm sure they are lovely and tastefully painted. Mine, unfortunately, were not. They were more of the airbrushed genre…and occasionally may have been encrusted with a gem or two. I know, I know, I can feel you judging me from here. In my defense, they were fiercely fabulous at the time. And although I have spent years enduring the endless ridicule of my sister and some close friends, at this moment, they came in handy.

ME: (with balls I didn't know I had) "I'm sorry, but perhaps you could skip your next nail appointment, and use that fifteen dollars to buy some school supplies for your child."

HER: "What?"

ME: "I used to have nails like that, too. It's about fifteen dollars to get them filled each time right? So you could use some of that money. I'd be more than happy to purchase the rest, but would really appreciate your help with collecting supplies for your child."

Maybe this wasn't my best move. I'm not exactly sending that positive karma out into the universe. But another year had begun.

SETTING: A BUSY city street outside of the subway entrance. Two teachers walk the few blocks from the subway to work. 7:15 a.m.

I felt lucky because I ran into my girlfriend and Super Colleague on the subway today. It always makes the commute easier when I have someone to chat with. You know, the death march I usually hear playing inside my head gets somewhat muffled when I can walk with a friend. Although, to be fair, sometimes it's not the death march but rather "Gangster's Paradise" or even Ludacris' "Runaway Love." On those days I feel like Michelle Pfeiffer in *Dangerous Minds* and I strut down the street. But most days, let's be real, it's damn early.

It was the first day of school. And we had both clearly selected our outfits with great care. An unsung bonus of the teaching profession is the ability to rationalize the need for new back-to-school clothes. Every year, despite the fact that I stopped growing years ago. You see, as I have said before, after a restful summer, I make many false promises to myself that this will be the year I look more "put together." Then I convince myself that my current wardrobe is all wrong and I *must* go shopping for strictly professional reasons.

As we stepped carefully over the discarded chicken bones and old hair extensions that litter the streets, we chatted about what we were planning for the first day. Now that I think about it, why don't we ever question the chicken bones *or* the hair extensions? I mean, that is not normal. Who is so desperate for a wing that they have to suck it down right there on the sidewalk and then throw it to the ground with a satisfied belch? Don't get me wrong, I loves me a good buffalo wing, but I usually like to wolf them down while sitting in some fab bar with my big old beer, all the while pretending that I'm really more into the veggies.

And the whole extension thing I can't even begin to understand because (1) I don't have them and (2) I do feel sorry for women with feminine balding. However, for some reason we step over all of this every morning without question, as if we were tiptoeing through the tulips or something.

*But...*we were about three blocks from school sipping on our hot bodega coffees when a plastic bag came floating through the air. Initially, we ignored it, chalking it up to the charm of our surroundings. But then, as if possessed, the bag followed us, forcing my girlfriend to bat it out of her face. Wait, let me say that again and then pause for dramatic effect. My Super Colleague batted garbage...that was floating through the air...out of her face.

(Pause.)

And that, my friends, is one gnarly, and very un-Michelle Pfeiffer–like, way to start the year.

"**G**OOD MORNING EVERYBODY!" A chorus of voices rises up to meet my greeting:

"Good morning Mrs. Mime."

"Good morning...what's her name again?"

"I'm hungry!"

"Good morning Mrs. Nini!"

"I need to go to the bathroom."

"My pencil is broken..."

"When is lunch?"

"He keeps looking at me! Stop!"

"Miss! Miss! I can't hold it!"

Another year has begun. And as I begin to break bad habits (read: spirits), refuse to tie shoes, and get 20 small people to say my name correctly, I can't believe this might be my last year in this place. I am going to miss it here.

I Love Naughty Boys

AFTER BEING IN school for what feels like a zillion years, I still get the first-day-of-school jitters. Usually this feeling manifests itself as an obsession with To Do lists of all kinds, a short temper with anyone I deem as someone who does not understand the pressures of teaching, and a single-minded determination to find the perfect first-day-of-school outfit.

You might wonder what makes me nervous after seven years of teaching. I should have this down by now, right? I know what to do. I know where I am going with my curriculum. I am familiar with my school and my colleagues (the good and the bad). I know where the bathroom is, even if I rarely get to use it. It's the kids that make me nervous, though; the kids are an unknown variable. I am always nervous that the upcoming year will be the year that I get a class from hell. The crazy thing is, I go through this every year. I get a nervous knot in my stomach starting around August 15. That knot promptly turns into full-blown anxiety as the first day approaches. From there, I predictably move into a period of mourning and irritation. I mourn my class from the previous year and feel irritated that I have to start all over with a new group of children who don't really get me…yet. Around November, I am usually totally in love with my class and wonder if any other class is quite as cute. I have never had a truly hellatious group of students. Never. On an arrogant day, I can convince myself that the reason I've never had a bad class is because I am so good at my job. But on my more honest days, I know I am just freaking lucky. So I guess you could say I'm always waiting for the other shoe to drop.

Logically, I use my anxiety to engage in a ridiculous number of "what-if" scenarios. What if I can't control them? What if we are all a bad mix? What if they hate me? What if I can't help them make enough progress?

And the big question…what if I don't have any fabulously naughty boys? Because I loves me the Naughty Boys!

Oh. Am I even allowed to say that? Please, people, let's keep it in context, shall we? When I say I love Naughty Boys, and believe me, I really do, I am talking about the type of challenging student that I relish. You may not know this (and many teachers out there won't admit it), but every teacher has her specialty, also known as her favorites.

Gasp! Yes, we have favorites! I will pause as you spend time wondering if *you* were ever one of the chosen for a former teacher…keep in mind, we don't all like the brownnosers. Unfortunately, I think I erred on the side of brownnoser when I was younger, which perhaps explains my slight aversion to similar little girls. One of the most horrifying moments of clarity I have ever had is when I realized that I was the type of brownnosing, overly anxious little girl that drives me nuts in my own classroom. In that moment of clarity when I realized how truly annoying I must have been, I swear I could hear a voice out there somewhere echoing, "Hey, you've got something brown on your face…" Whiney girls, criers, sneaks, chatty-chats-a-lot kids, the socially awkward…you name it and there is a teacher with a special place in her heart for that type of child. And thank goodness, right? Because someone has to love the whiney girls. For me, not so much…but the Naughty Boys, those are all mine. And the naughtier, the better.

I first realized my love for Naughty Boys during my third year of teaching. Oh, I had had run-ins with some very naughty friends during my first two years, but this was the first time one of them made me laugh out loud instead of run out of the room crying. (Okay, I never *really* ran out of the room...but I have spent some significant time crying over school drama in supply closets, bathroom stalls, and subway cars.)

The year I fell for the naughty ones was the year I had Glasses. I call him that because his were thick, always smeared with fingerprints, and perpetually crooked. It would almost seem cartoonish if it wasn't true. He was adorable! (The Naughty Ones usually are, you know.) But he was also like a bomb ready to explode: He had no control over his body whatsoever. This inability to sit still lead him to hit others for no apparent reason, fall out of his chair, call out during instruction, and hold the world record for least number of completed assignments. Ever.

He drove me insane. I tried keeping him inside for recess (holy backfire Batman, that kid needed to run around!), called his parents, put him on a sticker chart, yelled, reasoned, separated him from the group...you name it! And it was only the second week of school! Boyfriend could simply not get it together.

And then one day, the class was sitting on the carpet listening to a story. It was still early in the year, so everyone was in hard-core angel mode. Except my little friend. As I looked up from one of my favorite picture books, I caught a glimpse of Glasses in mid-backward somersault, or as my grandmother would say, he was ass over teakettle. She had a way with words. Yes, Glasses was doing a somersault. On my rug. While I was in the middle of a very dramatic reading of *Knuffle Bunny*, no less! He picked up so much momentum that he flipped all the way over, and then actually slid *underneath* the carpet. Yes, under it! I wanted to scream... but then his little head popped up from the floor, glasses askew, with the most thoroughly confused look on his face, as if he had never really seen me before and had no idea how he got under the rug in the first place. I couldn't bring myself to yell after that. Actually, it was all I could do to not laugh out loud.

Fast-forward to the end of the same day. Glasses is gyrating in his place, backpack on (remember that detail, it will be important later), ready to go home.

ME: "Glasses, please sit down, sweetie. School's not over yet."

HIM: "I can't, Mrs. Mimi, I can't find my backpack."

ME: (Wait a minute, isn't he *wearing* his backpack? It's the end of the day, Glasses, work with me!) "Um, honey, isn't it, um, on your back?"

HIM: "Huh?" (spinning around erratically like my beloved but somewhat dumb cat trying to catch her tail)

ME: "Sweetheart. Stop spinning, it's right there."

HIM: "I don't see it." (still spinning)

ME: (Please grant me patience...ten, nine, eight, seven...).
"Glasses, if you sit down, I promise you that you
will find that your backpack is indeed on your back
already."

HIM: "Okay." (Glasses then tries to sit down but after
spinning around like a top has virtually no balance
and ends up on his ass. Thank goodness his backpack
is right under it, or that might have hurt) "Oh! Mrs.
Mimi, I found it, don't worry! It was on the floor the
whole time."

And that's when I totally fell in love with Glasses.
Since then, I have always embraced the Naughty Boys,
who continue to be absolutely adorable and totally my
favorites.

His spinning didn't stop there either. Later, during my
third year of teaching, I had to videotape myself teaching a lesson and send it in to the Department of Education to prove that I was worthy of a tenured position.
Urban legend has it that no one actually watches these
tapes—and that one time a teacher sent in a recording
of a baseball game and still got tenure. But this could be
like the alligators who live in the sewer...

Anyhow, I had just taped my video and, against my better judgment, decided to watch it before sending it in, although my self-esteem probably would have been better served by *not* listening to my own voice on tape or seeing my back side on camera. As I cringed at my outfit choice, my eye was drawn to Glasses in the corner of the screen. At this point in the lesson, my back was turned to write something on the board. All my friends were seated on the carpet listening. Except for Glasses. He had been jangling around during the entire lesson, and, while I had my back turned, spun around in a full circle right there on the rug. At the time, I had no idea, but here was my evidence, right here on tape. I guess I could have punished him for being such a spaz on the carpet, but instead I found myself laughing out loud. I mean, this kid is literally vibrating through my entire lesson, manages to pull off some serious acrobatics behind my back, but still manages to raise his hand and answer questions.

Glasses and I managed to work together all year. I understood that he needed to tap, rattle, and shake everything in sight. In return, he seemed to understand that despite all his spinning, he needed to dig in and try. Glasses had a good year that year. And then he moved to Florida that June. I was heartbroken. I still wonder how he is doing and if he remembers me the way that I remember him.

I PARTICULARLY LIKE THOSE boys who come with some serious reputations. Keep in mind that I teach second grade, so coming in with a hard-core reputation makes you fairly badass in my mind. Sometimes I think these kids deserve to have their own soundtracks playing behind them as they cruise the hallways looking for trouble (and sometimes I think I should have my own soundtrack as I saunter down the street on my way to work...but that's another story). Rationally, it makes no sense that a seven-year-old child would arrive in a classroom with a rap sheet a mile long and permanently banned from gym, but schools are not always rational places.

At the end of each year, it has been somewhat of a tradition to sit with the previous year's teachers and let them elaborate on (read: "complain about") our incoming friends. The most puzzling part of this process, however, is that we never know exactly which kids are coming our way the following year. As a result, we have to listen to the teachers talk about *every single* child, none of whom we can connect to or picture in any real way. The process itself discourages any sort of productive, professional dialogue about transitioning children to the next grade. So really, what could be a very productive meeting in which the learning styles, preferences, and behaviors of children could be discussed and potentially matched to the perfect teacher rapidly deteriorates into what I like to think of as "Let's Complain About Our Former Kids to a Captive Audience and Watch Them Squirm."

PREVIOUS TEACHER #1: "Oh, and little Johnny? You'll never get him to do anything. He just rolls around the carpet and is completely incapable of sitting still."

ME: "Well, I had a child like that this year, and it really worked when I…"

PREVIOUS TEACHER #1: "Oh no. No. You couldn't possibly understand." (Please insert finger waving and some choruses of "mmmm-hmmm" from Previous Teacher #1's cronies here.) "He's awful. He will ruin your class. And his parents…well…they…"

Why is it that former teachers love to horrify future teachers with outrageous stories of misbehavior rather than words of encouragement anyway? Aren't we all on the same team? And it is at this point in the conversation that I tune out and start thinking about summer plans, or what I'm going to wear tomorrow. The funny thing is, I think that these types of Previous Teachers have good intentions. Perhaps they wished they had been warned. Or maybe they just need to get it all off their chests, because no one else would listen when they really needed help.

Oh, and then after all that, everything the teachers said is disregarded, and the kids are randomly placed on new class lists, which are then randomly assigned to each teacher. Brilliant system, eh?

I am always filled with anxiety and dread as I scan down my list of incoming students. You know, because it was so thoughtfully prepared? I try desperately to recall the stories from the Tirade of the Previous Teachers, but usually can't. However, some children, the few and the bold, don't even need an introduction. I've already heard their names whispered in furious tones, screamed down the hallways, and complained about around the micro-wave... and about the time they told The Weave to go F herself. (Ballsy, no? Seriously, bad boys are fab!) The special place I have in my heart for these Naughty Boys urges me to give them a clean slate, allowing them to begin again, at the ripe old age of seven. Plus, I have found that not knowing all the gory details equals fewer nightmares over the summer. Knowing the gory details usually equals many, many (seriously, a lot of) fruity cocktails imbibed in an effort to get my mind to stop rac-ing with visions of chairs being thrown across the room. Remember, I said I *liked* Naughty Boys...but even I get nervous when I'm presented with a whopper.

I have a theory that each grade level team should be comprised of teachers who have very different Kid

Specialties. That way, there is someone for everyone. My team is, therefore, perfect in my mind. I have one Super Colleague who loves noisy, busy kids. There is way too much moving around and scraps of paper all over the floor for me, but it works for her. My other Super Colleague likes super girly girls, and is traumatized when one of them farts or burps, which I find hysterical. And the last Super Colleague on the team likes the whiney girls. After all, somebody has to. For five years, she and I worked across the hall from each other and I think it was a match made in heaven. First of all, it was wonderful to have someone to turn to for advice with the whiney ones in my class so I didn't start poking my eyes out every time they cried. And second of all, it was *hysterical* to watch her deal with her Naughty Boys. Because although each teacher has her specialty, there is also another type of child who drives her nuts and always seems to be able to make her question her qualifications for teaching in the first place. That type of child is like kryptonite for teachers. For my Super Colleague across the hall, Naughty Boys were just not her thing.

Throughout the years, she dealt with some real winners. One year she had a child rolling around at the back of the classroom flinging cubes at the rest of the class seated on the carpet. Then there was the time she had two friends flipping each other the bird across the room. Those are among some of the highlights. And then...

It was October, a time of the year when most of your class has settled beautifully into a productive routine. However, October is also a time when those who have ants in their pants, meaning my beloved Naughty Boys, get a little itchy and start to really show their bad-boy stuff. My Super Colleague had been dealing with one little boy who we will call Locks. He had long, beautiful, possibly flat-ironed hair to his waist. Perhaps he was naughty because at certain angles, he looked like a little girl...hmmm. Locks called out, hit others, started fights, threw things, never did any work, and generally threw off any of the flow the teacher had established in the classroom. Any teacher, even those of us who relish the challenge of Naughty Boys, would have a hard time dealing with children who disrupt the learning of everyone else. It's just not fair, no matter how you look at it.

One day, Locks pushed my Super Colleague too far. It was Writer's Workshop in both of our classrooms—an oasis of calm, quiet focus in the midst of the afternoon. This was, hands down, my Super Colleague's favorite part of the day. Locks was in rare form. From across the hallway, I could hear him desperately trying to disrupt the children around him and ruin this sacred time of day. At first, my Super Colleague was the picture of patience, quietly reminding him to sit in his seat, remember that he was part of a community...blah blah blah. I don't know exactly what the last straw was, but I was conferencing with one of my friends near the open door of my class-room when I heard the words "That's it!" shouted from across the hall.

"Oooo…this is going to be good," I thought to myself (professional, I know).

As I looked up, I saw my Super Colleague, her face twisted into a snarl, eyebrows knitted together, and eyes like slits, pushing, yes pushing, Locks down the hall in his chair.

Stop for a minute and try to picture this. She just gets up, takes the back of his chair and begins pushing him out of the classroom and down the hall. Brilliant!

Locks is so shocked to be moving at all that he stayed seated until the ride was over.

I think she only pushed him down the hall and left him outside the door of another Super Colleague. But I realized then that the kryptonite child can push you to your limits, making you do things you never imag-ined yourself doing as a teacher. Nothing horribly mean, unforgivable, or illegal, but just crazy enough to make you question your own sanity.

Y ALL-TIME Baddest-Badass-Boy was a trip. Stories of *his* adventures in kindergarten had somehow floated up to my floor and horrified all of us: rolling around on the carpet, kicking other children, cursing, refusing to do work, running away from the teacher, and, as the icing on the cake, frequent incidents in which he told The Weave where she could shove it.

He was like my dream child.

All year we worked on harnessing his energy so that he could focus in class, complete his work, and learn to interact with everyone in more positive ways. And before I knew it, my little friend was like a new man. I mean, yes, he still hit kids at recess occasionally and got in trouble for throwing things at lunch, but if you saw what they served my poor friends, you might want to throw it across the room, too. But despite all that, he worked *hard*. And no matter how many little setbacks a kid might have, I have to respect that. For some kids it's easy to do the right thing, and good for them, they're lucky. But for others, it is a constant battle with their inner-naughty selves, and I think that that kind of focus and self-control deserves to be recognized.

On the last day of school, he quietly came back into

my classroom after they had been dismissed for the last time, gave me a giant bear hug, and said, "I love you, Mrs. Mimi." It was all I could do to hold back the tears until he left the room.

W HILE I LOVE to celebrate my triumphs and regale people with tales of my successes, I believe it is character building for each teacher to recognize her weak points. I do not think that cheapens my status as an Educational Rock Star at all. Here are my faults, in no particular order: I almost never remember to add the numbers on the calendar each day and I usually stop updating our daily schedule sometime during the third week of school. Sometimes, I throw out homework packets because I just can't deal with correcting them that week. I have to force myself to love social studies (I mean, we study "urban, rural, and suburban community" for like four months...it's brutal). And my least favorite kind of student is a whiney and dishonest girl. (Insert ominous music, like that music they play at the end of every segment of *The Hills* to let you know some serious stuff is going to go down after the break.) At this point you might want to add "watches bad television" to my list of flaws.

Be warned. Whiney and dishonest girls can be the pits. There are moments, yes, when I love them, but only because I work very hard to find something to love about each child. With whiney/dishonest girls, sometimes I am hanging on by a thread (like "she wears cute shirts" or "I love her because her desk is organized").

Last year I had one girl who trumped all the whiney/dishonest girls I have ever taught. I will refer to her here as The Vagina Monologues. (At this point, you might want to start humming "Let's Talk About Sex" by Salt N Pepa in your head, because it would be a fitting addition to my personal soundtrack at this point.)

Yes, let's talk about all the good things and the bad things that may be.

Although I'd rather not. Why? you ask. Because talking about sex, lesbianism, and rape with eight-year-old children just seems wrong. I mean, make your own parenting decisions, but to me, this is not something I ever thought I would be talking about in school when I signed up to be an early elementary school teacher. They (and I'm not sure who I mean by "they" except for some-one more powerful and all-knowing than myself) should warn you at the door as you try to skip inside armed with only bags full of stickers and rainbow dreams.

As I have said before, it is NOT all flowers and sausages, people. Right now, you may be thinking, "What the heck is she talking about? Sex? Lesbianism? Sausages?"

But you're intrigued, right? Don't act like you're not.

I am talking about The Vagina Monologues, a little girl who forced me to cover the above issues in my classroom. You see, that year there had been a lot of dirty talk on the playground, all of which was instigated and encouraged by The Vagina Monologues. I am a firm believer of "a time and place for everything," but I do not think that recess is the time. Nor do I believe that the playground is the place to be discussing things of this nature. Why, oh why aren't they talking about crayons, freeze tag, and Popsicles? I'm pretty sure that was my conversational repertoire as a child.

Here are some examples of the recent "dirty talk" which spread like wild fire across the lower grade playground:

"Your mom has sex on you."

"You want to have sex on your uncle."

"He is going to rape on you."

And the ever popular "Your pussy smells."

Whoever came up with the phrase "from the lips of children" evidently never hung out on the playground at recess. Friends, I had no idea what to do with this situation. My kryptonite, this whiney/dishonest girl turned insane dirty talker, had truly thrown me for a loop. I mean, I thought my class was so sweet. I really and truly loved that class. And not in that phony Little Miss Sunshine, I Have to Love My Class Because That Is What Teachers Are Supposed to Say way…I mean, I honestly missed them a little over school breaks. Somehow I managed to continue to sip on a fabulous cocktail or two during said breaks—but still, I thought about them all the same.

When I was their age (when I walked uphill to and from school…) the boys were infested with cooties, pussies were *cats,* and we NEVER discussed a foul bodily odor other than the occasional fart. So, I guess farting was the most risque topic we covered. Farting and perhaps, just perhaps, we would try out a curse word or two. But we certainly did not discuss explicit sexual acts, nor do I think I had ever even heard of rape. The whole notion of French kissing was still up for debate.

In sum, we were not this knowledgeable.

By the way, I *never* thought I would talk like this about my own childhood…seriously, I sound like my mom when she regales me with tales of her childhood. I totally promised myself that I would refrain from starting sentences with phrases such as "When I was little…" or "In my day…" Well, friends, I am a true disappointment in that sense as I have fallen down that slippery slope. All of which probably means that I am (sigh) old. I also never thought that I would have to prepare a lesson on "dirty talk" for my early elementary class. Or would be forced to pee in a bathroom infested with mice, but that's another story.

But it was all out there now, and The Vagina Monologues couldn't take it back. It's not like when kids accidentally call me "mom" and then blush furiously as we both pretend it didn't happen. Or when they let a fart fly on the carpet in the middle of a read aloud and we all try our darndest to ignore it.

No, it was out there and I had to deal with it. I couldn't have my friends using these words or thinking it is okay to use them in these ways. And, clearly they were being exposed to these ideas somewhere and I couldn't let them be filled with all this misinformation, right? So I teamed up with one of my colleagues and we planned a whole little talk on Words They Might Hear on the Playground That Could Make Them Uncomfortable and discussed the proper time to think and talk about those things. We also wrote a letter home explaining the entire situation to parents, reassuring them that this Little Talk would not turn into Sex Ed.

So for any of you out there who *still* think this job is a cake walk, who *still* believe that all I do is finger paint and lead sing-a-longs, and who *still* insist that small children are just adorable—put that in your pipe and smoke it.

Although, I secretly wished that we *could* just sing songs, and finger paint this one away.

IT'S SIX WEEKS into the school year, and I don't know if I like them. Was that out loud? Am I going to get struck by lightning? The last few weeks have been...hard.

I can't believe I just admitted that! But it's totally true. I don't know what happened. I feel like I spend all my time breaking bad habits—shouting out, getting up out of the seat, yelling at one another, not listening, scribbling down work to be finished first. I know that doesn't sound so shocking; however, may I remind you that it has been only a few weeks? Children are supposed to be in their end-of-the-summer/beginning-of-the-school-year comas. They're supposed to be a little bit nervous. They're supposed to be...quiet. At least for the first few days, right?

But, oh, there has been no quiet. And the child that was rumored to be the Naughtiest Naughty Boy of all time is...mean. Just mean to other children. Which is so not cute.

Mr. Mimi says that I am insanely predictable and go through this every year. I prefer to think of myself as a woman of mystery and intrigue, but whatever. He adds that by November I will be in love with my class and everything will be fine.

But I don't know. Maybe this is my sign to go. My time in this school is up. Right? I don't want to become burned out and angry. At the kids anyway. I've been burned out and angry with administrative bullshit for years, but the kids...I always love the kids. Don't I?

The next couple of weeks felt like a battle. A battle between me and every bad habit I have ever had to confront. Topped off with the fact that my group is way behind grade level in many ways, I feel like I am at the bottom of Mount Everest, armed only with a pair of fabulous high heels and one bottle of water. And we all know I don't hike. In other words, I'm screwed.

Some of my feelings of screwed-ness are selfish. I mean, I'm thinking about leaving and I can't go out like this. I need to end on a high note, loving my class and feeling like my decision was a necessary career move rather than me running out with my tail between my legs, admitting defeat. There are certain stereotypes of urban schoolteachers that I am vehemently opposed to. Those images, as I have said before, usually include abnormal amounts of leather clothing and Michelle Pfeiffer. But then there is also the image of the teacher who couldn't hack it in the inner city—and I desperately need to not be that girl.

Other feelings of screwed-ness are focused more professionally on the kids. I mean, we have a *long* way to go before they are ready for third grade and let's be real, the amount of actual support I receive from outside sources is minuscule. Most days it feels as if our "support staff" is working against me, challenging me to some sort of screwed up Educational Endurance Challenge. In all honesty, I receive more support from a good bra.

My usual back-to-school high is fading. Fast.

I'm beginning to feel like every night I go home and have to psych myself up for the next day. In the past, my alarm clock would go off at the ungodly hour of 5:15 and after several disoriented minutes of hating my life, I would get up and actually look forward to going in to work and seeing my little friends. I mean, cut me some slack here, I'm not exactly my sweetest first thing in the morning. (Mr. Mimi has said many times that no one would ever call me "sweet.") But recently when the alarm clock goes off, I feel nothing except a general dislike of alarm clocks. In the shower, I give myself pep talks, convincing myself that today will be different. We will begin to make real progress. My class will start to resemble the sort of positive community that I have prided myself on for years. I have to fight back the growing fear that I'm burned out, and on my way to Angry Teacher Who Should Just Quit Land. I mean, that's a hop, skip, and a jump from Macaroni-Necklace and Themed-Earring World, a fate I would like to avoid if possible. For some people, that totally works, but those looks so don't go with my shoes.

A
S HALLOWEEN APPROACHED, things started to get better. My friends *finally* seemed to be settling into some sort of a routine and were beginning to understand how things work in Mrs. Mimi's world. Kids started to work together instead of fight and the quality of their work began to improve. I was seeing some growth academically, too, which made me feel a bit better. Now, let's not get carried away here. Life wasn't all flowers and sausages in my room—far from it. Honestly, I don't think I would want to teach in a classroom where all the children were so well behaved that the room feels sterile. I like a little sauciness in my day. And while things were moving along nicely, I still hadn't found my lovable Naughty Boy to help me get through the year.

Enter Curly.

Now, Curly had been in my room all along. He has

always been very cute to look at—crazy curls, big brown eyes, and a devilish little smile. But, earlier in the year, I had found him to be either irritating (he was one of those who followed me around the classroom for attention) or totally disengaged. Maybe he was just feeling me out or maybe he was testing me. I don't know. Evidently I must have passed.

At this point in the year, I insist that my friends write both their first and last name at the top of their papers. It may not sound like a big deal, but boy did I rock their world with that one! It was like I asked them to write 500 pages on their summer vacation or something. Evidently, writing one's first and last name is very painful.

However, I don't care (that's the caring teacher in me). Personally, I think that they balked at me because many of them don't know how to spell their last name confidently (a.k.a. without sneaking a peek at the nametag taped to their desk). I figure it is the least I can do for them.

I have just finished my "gentle reminder" to write first and last names before papers are collected when I notice my little friend Curly, who is sitting right in front of me, fails to even make a move for his pencil.

Pardon me? I have spoken, friend…

ME: "Um, Curly? Last name…I know you heard me…"

HIM: "I only have one name."

ME: "What?"

HIM: "I'm not using my last name anymore."

ME: "Who are you, Cher?"

HIM: (blank stare)

ME: (I am so old.) "What do you mean?"

HIM: "I'm like Fitty." (translation: that is Fifty to most of us)

ME: "I see. Well even *he* has a last name."

HIM: (blank stare)

ME: "Cent." (Ha! What do you say to that, little friend? Not so old after all…)

It got me thinking, though. I recently got married, so my last name is currently up for debate at work. I legally changed my name but that doesn't stop everyone from constantly referring to me by my maiden name, a jacked up version of my married name, or some sort of weird hybrid of the two. But what if I had only one name? Like Fabulous. Or Oh Wise One (I guess that's three names). Maybe something with one syllable, like Star.

Something to think about…

AND THEN I HAD the moment I had been waiting for. The moment when I knew that this new class and I would be okay. It was the moment when I got all Mama Bear and defended my friends in the face of all the ridiculousness out there.

Curly came in after recess one day very upset. He informed me that the class would be losing recess for an entire week. And that as punishment, they were supposed to bring their books outside and read. Reading as punishment. Fantastic.

I love to read. I want my students to love to read, but I know that reading can be hard. It's hard to teach, too. We can't always tell what's going on in that little head or determine what is the best way to help. I try really hard to make sure my students have something they find *worth* reading, too, because there is nothing worse than struggling through something hard that you don't care about either. (Believe me, if I didn't care about my job or my students, it would *not* be worth the struggle.) So, I let them read newspapers, magazines, nonfiction, fiction...whatever...just read something! With some friends it's working, with others...they still look at me like I'm crazy when it's private reading time (sigh).

So you can imagine how *pissed* I was when Curly shared this little tidbit with me. There are so many problems here, I don't even know where to start.

1. First of all, a *whole week* (for everyone) without recess...ridiculous.

2. Reading as a punishment. Dude. Duuuuuude. Why are you doing this to me? To them? How do you think my little strugglers are going to take to finding a good book now?

3. Do you have any idea, recess ladies, how many books we are going to *lose*? They don't grow on trees, you know.

4. What about the idea of "logical consequences"? Anyone? Anyone? No? Or the kids who really weren't doing anything wrong or even know what happened?

I went to the recess ladies and pled my case. I told them that while I understood that some of the children needed to be punished for their behavior, making them read as punishment was not the answer. Instead, I offered to take the offenders for that entire week and hold them in my classroom. Because losing recess and reflecting on what you've done sounds a bit more logical, to me at least.

Clearly ambivalent, the recess ladies gave me the

names of the wrong doers and everyone else was free to go. After recess the next day, Curly came up to me and said, "Mrs. Mimi, we make a good team."

Yeah, we do.

Somebody, Go Get Me a Soapbox!

*L*ET THE TITLE of this section be a bit of a warning to you, dear reader…for Mrs. Mimi is angry. Angry and sick of egg timers, arrogant clipboard-wielding nonteachers and Number 2 pencils!

I have finally emerged from that Black Hole that is the beginning of the year and realized that it is November. I have no idea what happened to October. I think it might have passed in a haze of sleeplessness, or perhaps it was simply consumed by the barrage of tests I am required to administer. Weeks come and go, seasons change, and all of a sudden, it's November and all I have to show for it is a big old pile o' data. (Okay, it's not really *all* I have, but seriously, the amount of testing I subject my little friends to is downright ridiculous.) Now some people may look at that big old pile of numbers and graphs and think, "Wow, she has been teaching her hiney off!" I am not one of those people. I look at that big old pile of paper and wonder what I've really accomplished (and secretly worry that somewhere the rain forest is crying).

Now, when I got into teaching, I knew I would have to wear many hats. I think that part is fairly obvious. Sometimes I am a mommy, sometimes I am a social worker, sometimes I am a coach, sometimes I am a tyrant, and sometimes I get to teach. However, my college professors neglected to inform me that many times (not just sometimes) I would also be expected to play the role of data analyst, performing such mundane tasks as data collection, data input, data transfer, and the ever popular data analysis. Now, don't get me wrong, I love a good checklist. I think I have made my love of lists of all kinds fairly clear. I take great pride in useful checklists that give me a quick glance at my students' progress and help me to see who needs additional help in certain areas. Yes, in that sense, checklists are the bomb. If this was always the case, I would happily check myself off into an oblivion. Yet, sadly, this is not always the case.

Please keep in mind that I do not teach a testing grade. For those of you nonteachers out there, testing grades are the years in which children are subjected to intense state exams in areas such as math and language. Hallelujah that I don't have to add *that* to my plate. So I'm not even talking about the All Powerful Standardized Test, which has been made a household name thanks to it's overuse and an immense amount of media coverage. No, I will not be discussing *those* types of assessments here. Rather, I will be discussing (read: venting, or perhaps more accurately, whining about) *all the other tests* that children (and teachers) are subjected to, yet are often *not* discussed in a public forum. Usually these tests are only discussed in angry hushed tones by other teachers over a hastily microwaved lunch of leftovers or the always classic PB and J. However, today, friends, today I hope to blow this topic wide open and start a much more public conversation. (And then I will patiently wait for Oprah to call and the subsequent massive amounts of media coverage, because this is some shocking stuff!)

Regrettably, I think my philosophy of testing differs from the philosophy held by the powers that be. And really, do you think my philosophy matters to any of them? I will share it with you regardless. You see, a wise person once told me that the best test preparation is actually teaching students deeply and using thoughtful assessments to guide that teaching. Genius, right? If we spent more time actually teaching in meaningful ways, and less time shuffling numbers around, then perhaps our friends would be more adequately prepared. You know, for life and stuff...oh and tests I guess.

Unfortunately, wise people rarely get listened to in schools. Instead we are now testing the living crap out of our children, rather than teaching the living crap out of them. There really isn't a more gentle way to put it. Evidently simply administering *more* tests equates to actually *preparing* for the test in some people's book. Let me repeat, that's not true in my book, but who cares about my book? (Besides Oprah, that is. Seriously, call me!) So despite my constant protests, I must give my children roughly ten million tests over the course of second grade. Okay, maybe I'm exaggerating a tad, but honestly, I think we might be one small step away from prodding kids with hot pokers to see if they know how to skip count by fives. That's how insane the testing has become...seriously, hot pokers and maybe a full body scan, you know, just for ha-has. At this point, I wouldn't be surprised if someone told me I had to stick thermometers up all their little behinds and record the temperature. On six separate data sheets. And on two different charts. In triplicate.

So, despite much of our better judgment, we collect data about everything whether it's useful or not. I have wondered from time to time if the department of education has an odd graphing fetish, or maybe gets off on tallying stuff, but I have a feeling that secretly, all those numbers and charts just make them feel more important and give them a false sense of progress. Maybe that's how they sleep at night…with visions of graphs dancing in their heads.

To give you an inkling of just how out of control this has gotten, let me tell you about the assessments I am forced (excuse me, was that out loud…again?), I meant *privileged* to give to my students. So for a moment, please pardon the teacher-speak.

By the end of October I will have given my friends no fewer than seven tests in the area of literacy alone. My little friends will be forced to read lists of words, write a short personal narrative, read books out loud, and take several spelling tests. I will then take all of this information and dutifully plot it on various graphs, checklists, and data sheets. Buried behind my mound of paperwork, I am rendered almost unrecognizable, except for the fabulous pair of shoes peeking out from underneath the mountain of data. But that is not all—oh no, far from it! We then need to move on to math. Gotta hit the three Rs, right? In addition to jumping through hoops set ablaze, I will subject my friends to a math interview, a battery of preassessments, and several hands-on problem-solving activities. As they are furiously computing, I walk around the classroom and feverishly record their every move on an extensive checklist. These checks will then be transferred to several graphs, all of which are emailed off to the administration as proof that I am, indeed, doing my job. Oddly, though, I am left to wonder how this obsession with testing and data collection became the defining feature of my job.

Is that gross or what? Pretty soon we're going to be assessing them on how thoroughly they wipe after a trip to the bathroom. Or maybe we'll have to start using a rubric to score their ability to open their milk cartons at lunch. Perhaps we should think about attaching a bubble sheet to their recess routine just to make sure that their free play is highly monitored and accounted for.

I keep waiting for their little turkey timers to pop. They have to be done. I know I am. And while I feel sorry for my little friends, we also need to recognize the toll all of this testing takes on teachers. Or really, the toll it takes on *me,* because it's all about me, isn't it?

You see, all of this testing is *killing* my inner teacher. I mean in math alone we waste four or five instructional days *every month* testing the kids. That's 25 percent of the month. I'll wait while you let the ridiculousness and enormity of that last statement sink in. (Insert me running for a cocktail to wave around whilst standing upon my soapbox and continuing my rant on testing, hence giving you enough time to let your mouth hang open in utter shock at how much potential instructional time is devoted to tests that don't necessarily help said instruction.) It's getting to the point where there is so little time in between tests that I'm not really sure what we have had the time to actually do anything that is worth testing. (Cocktail sloshing here.)

In the spirit of Extreme Standardized Testing (insert sarcastic tone here, and maybe a small tear running down my cheek), there is one individual at my school who has taken it upon herself to develop a whole *new* test (insert exaggerated fist pumping—Yes! More tests!) that duplicates some of the findings of our existing tests and impacts my instruction in no way at all. She has also found a way to make the test a degrading experience for teachers. Jackpot, right? This ray of sunshine can also be referred to as The Bacon Hunter. If I was going to be a superhero (fingers crossed), she would be my archenemy. Who is The Bacon Hunter you ask? What an excellent question! Let me pause and introduce this "colleague" of mine. The Bacon Hunter is one of our in-house staff developers. In theory, it sounds like a great premise to have someone on staff who supports teachers in their learning as well as in their ability to translate that learning into direct results for children. Ah, but there is the rub, my friends: Don't let the title "staff developer" fool you. There is no development going on, at least not because of anything that *this* individual is doing. Unless you consider the possibility that she was hired to develop into a *huge* pain in the arse for teachers. Then yes, there is definitely development going on in that sense.

I lovingly call her The Bacon Hunter because of her grueling daily schedule, which appears to revolve around bacon. Let's see, each day she arrives approximately ten minutes late to work, then she proceeds with the exhausting task of ordering her daily bacon, egg, and cheese sandwich, which is followed by eating said sandwich, after which she moves on to looking for potential bacon crumbs on her desk. Maybe I'm not cutting her enough slack. After all, it must be terribly difficult to place long and complicated breakfast orders each and every morning from 8:00 to 8:45 while the rest of us are teaching. And then you have to wait for the order, count out money, and figure out a tip.

So, keep in mind that we are already assessing children on the various math standards about 400 other ways that are more authentic than her poorly designed pen-to-paper–test. For example, I keep anecdotal notes about each child's work in certain areas as I circulate around the room or pull a small group. But, I guess my "soft data" isn't as valuable as hard numbers. Maybe if I wrote it in binary code? Or morse code? So, we are mandated to give this additional assessment, created by The Bacon Hunter herself, about once a month. So not only is it unnecessary, it's basically omnipresent. As icing on the cake, she also demands (read: wields her nonexistent authority) that we turn the completed test in to her so *she* can grade them. And there, my friends, we have that extraspecial slap in the face to teachers.

Because of course I can't be expected to draw the hands on a clock correctly.

Or add double-digit numbers.

Or measure a straight line to the nearest inch.

I mean, those who can't do, teach, right?

Aaaaahhhhhhh!

Are you kidding me? I can't correct my own students' *work*? So not only does she waste my/our time by insisting that we engage in this ridiculousness, she also succeeds in insulting our intelligence and maintains her position as a raging jerk off.

Sah-weet.

The Bacon Hunter has corrected and photocopied the most recent Assessment of Nothing she created and has demanded (read: snarled) that it be distributed to parents.

"And I will be checking up on you," she threatened.

I am evidently no smarter or more responsible than

the children I teach. Oh, and apparently I respond to threats, too.

In the spirit of Being Positive in 2008, I decided not to fight this battle at this point in time. I mean, a girl can only handle so much.

A few weeks later, I am having a meeting with Chubby Cheeks' mom and dutifully hand her The Bacon Hunter's incoherent test along with a bunch of my own data. (I am such a sheep sometimes.) This particularly motivated and concerned parent (yes, friends, they are out there and I love them) took the time to look through the test, which is something I had failed to do because as I have said before, the test is worthless to my instruction. Oh, and the kids took it like two months ago, but I just got them back today. Nice work, Bacon Hunter!

CONCERNED PARENT: "Mrs. Mimi, why was this marked wrong?"

ME: (looking at the paper and seeing that the child has written $6 \times 3 = 18$ in response to a number story, which is, duh, correct) "Uuuhhhhh...I'm not sure."

CONCERNED PARENT: "Didn't you correct this test?"

ME: (Shit. I am not covering for this woman.) "No."

CONCERNED PARENT: "Who did?"

ME: "Our math specialist."

CONCERNED PARENT: "And, isn't this also correct?"

ME: (looking at the paper once again, seeing 22 + 15 = 37, which is, yet again, correct.) "Um, yes it is."

CONCERNED PARENT: "Actually it looks like my son should have gotten several of these marked correct."

ME: "Yes, it does."

CONCERNED PARENT: "What does your math specialist do with the results of this test?"

ME: "She graphs the information for the entire grade and then it is placed in the kids' math portfolio. The Visionary gets a copy as well."

CONCERNED PARENT: "And it's incorrect?"

ME: "Um, yes. Again, I'm very sorry. Please know that I plan instruction and grade your child based on assessments I create, assign, and grade myself. While this test is required, I rely more on the notes I take as children are actually engaged in math work."

CONCERNED PARENT: "I am sure that you do. I have a lot of confidence in your work. My son has been making a lot of progress this year. But don't you think I should bring these errors on the part of your math specialist to the attention of the principal? I mean, this is more than just one mistake and it's in Chubby Cheeks' portfolio."

ME: "Yes, yes, I do think he would be interested. Let me

walk you down to his office. I think he would like to hear it from you himself."

Is it wrong that I smiled from ear to ear the entire walk down the stairs?

———————————— ⟨rat⟩ ————————————

A S I WAS saying before, all this testing doesn't just effect the children. Oh no, because they are not the *only ones* being tested. Teachers are being tested, too. Our test is to see how adequately we can prepare our friends for this barrage of Scan Tron sheets and Number 2 pencils. Perhaps these tests aren't what one would consider a conventional test of intelligence; they are more a test of compliance than anything else. Evidently, compliance equals good teaching. I learned *that* lesson a long time ago.

In the early days of my teaching career I was handed two items and told that they were absolutely essential to my success as a teacher (if you define a successful teacher by their students' test scores alone, that is). These items were an egg timer and a diagram of a wall. Yes, friends, an egg timer and a diagram of a wall were going to be the two precious tools with which I would take second grade by storm.

The egg timer was intended to keep me on track. "Task on time" was a lovely phrase coined by one of my administrators to describe this very important test of my ability as a teacher. If I was to pass the Big Teacher Test, I was to remain task on time at all times. For those of you who aren't privy to such militant terminology, "task on time" simply means that I am doing exactly what my schedule says I should be doing at all times. ALL TIMES. "Sorry if you need to go to the bathroom, boys and girls!"

"You threw up in the back of the room, sweetheart...can it wait?"

"Hey, friend, the timer is about to go off, can we talk about your parents' divorce later? Just stop crying for now."

You see, we all had egg timers. Up and down the hallway, at precisely 9:10, you could hear egg timers going off in perfect unison, a symphony devoted to the importance of task on time. As those bells joyfully rang out, teachers everywhere could be seen frantically moving to the next prescribed activity. To hell with student understanding! Be gone, thoroughly completed tasks! The bell has rung, and it is time to move on. And as the day rolled on, punctuated by the piercing cries of the egg timer, teachers scrambled frantically to just keep up and pass the test.

As I said before, we were also given diagrams of a wall. These diagrams detailed every chart, poster, and scrap of paper to be hung on the chalkboard at the front of the room. For example, the alphabet poster had to be precisely three inches to the left of the strategy chart, which was to be hung over the teacher's chair for optimal learning to occur. This test of a teacher's ability to follow directions, measure, and decipher a key was crucial. Or so we were told.

Exactly *how* were our abilities assessed you ask? What a fabulous question! Well, every so often, a group of people in suits, forgive me if I don't remember their names for they never actually worked in the school building, would come around armed with clipboards. These clipboards contained checklist after checklist. I was never allowed to see any of these precious checklists (I mean, why give us any feedback, right?), so I can only imagine some of the items that were potentially listed. Let's see, "Teacher sits with right leg crossed over left." Check! "Reading banner is hung five inches to the right of word wall and has yellow lettering." Check! "Bell rings, teacher salivates." Check!

Fortunately, we are no longer subjected to the people in suits with clipboards. We must have passed *that* test, I guess. However, this obsession with controlling everything, and I mean *everything*, has prevailed in the minds of some of my colleagues. Maybe at one time they were capable of thinking for themselves and valuing the individual touches that each teacher can bring to her classroom, but now, not so much. All I know is that now, there are many ridiculous demands placed on teachers in the name of testing our compliance. Or patience. Same thing, right?

For example, insisting that all of us have the exact same bathroom pass appears to be of the utmost importance. Mandating that each teacher display his or her reading group schedule the same way is essential. Remaining resolute in the demand for each teacher to use the exact same colors on her behavior chart? Fundamental. Call me crazy, but I might have chosen different battles.

ITHIN THE LAST couple of years, after the novelty of seeing teachers jump at the sound of a bell had worn off, someone had the genius idea to put a great deal of our tests on a handheld computer. When we were first presented with our little Palm Pilots, I thought to myself, "Self, hey, these are pretty snazzy! This will be fabulous!" I was suddenly filled with a renewed hope for the beginning of the year. Maybe I wouldn't have to spend quite so many hours at home feverishly transferring individual results to larger charts of class progress.

However, as I whipped out my stylus and set to work tapping away as my friends plowed through list after list of words, I quickly realized that this new technology had the potential to push me over the edge. I mean, now the timer wasn't ticking away from the top of the bookshelf, it was ticking away *right in front of my eyes!* It was like the countdown to watching a bomb explode. Or my head. You pick. You see, each of my friends needed to be timed, to see how many words they could read in a minute. But, as I was about to find out, this technological advancement appeared to more adequately assess my ability to accurately tap away at a touch screen than my friends' ability to read a list of words in a given amount of time.

FRIEND: (reading from a list) "Have, has, had, been, people down..."

ME: (frantically tapping incorrect responses on my little handheld...Wait a minute, why isn't anything happening??!)

FRIEND: "Long, after, called, special, idea, behind..."

ME: (visibly sweating) (*Where did this kid learn how to read so fast? Shit, slow down, honey, I'm tapping my little heart out!*) (tap, tap, tappity, tap)

FRIEND: "after, always, usually..."

ME: (At this point, I am about ten words behind and

am desperately trying to keep up. I have also sweat through my shirt.) "What did you say, honey?" *(What was wrong with circling the wrong answer with a pencil anyway? Freaking technology...)*

As my friend finished reading his list and I silently cursed the unreliable touch screen, I wondered if I had even tapped accurately and if the dry cleaner was going to be able to do anything about my shirt. That was intense! I couldn't seem to tap fast enough. I mean, what is really being tested here? My friends' ability to read or my ability to tap at a screen? Their reading accuracy or my anti-perspirant?

Later that day, exhausted from my excessive stylus workout, I decided to revel in the fruits of my labor by synching my handheld to the computer and printing out graph after glorious graph (made all the more glorious by the mere fact that I didn't have to make them myself!). As I hooked up the cord and pressed the magical button to synch, I checked my email.

You have *got* to be kidding me.

Dear Teachers,

Please print out all data from your Palm Pilots. Then transfer all the data to the checklists we used last year. These are much easier for me to read. I need three copies in my box by the end of the day.

The Weave

It was then that I began to fantasize about the physical harm one could cause armed only with a tap-happy stylus.

F I HAVE learned anything about teaching in my short time in the classroom, it is that a teacher has to be willing to constantly reinvent herself, finding ways to stay positive and motivated. For me, the simple act of turning the page in my planner can refresh my attitude. Other times, I need a big old cocktail. I have even fantasized about keeping a blender and margarita fixings in the back of my room...for after school, of course. And I said "fantasize": I don't actually have one. Relax.

I know I have to get over this testing thing. So I think, "Self, if you have to give all these freaking tests, at least try to put them to good use." After a few weeks of thinking, I decide that it might be beneficial for my students to use all this testing data to create goals for their own learning in math. In the past, I filed their tests for my own purposes and didn't bother showing them how they did. Because, really, most of the information is used to help me tailor my instruction, and shouldn't be used to make them feel bad when they do poorly. And the rest of it is just useless. Maybe I'm babying them, but there's something to be said about preserving their little egos.

So, I start passing back their corrected tests (the ones I'm allowed to correct, that is). It's all done very privately and after a discussion of what it means to be honest about our strengths and weaknesses. Using their tests, I ask each child to write down on an index card one thing they noticed they are good at and one thing they noticed they need help with. Then we bring our strengths and weaknesses to the carpet and share them. That way I can reinforce the idea that *everyone* has something they can get better at, as well as establish a network of experts that students can go to for help if I am busy with another child. It seems to work pretty well. We start repeating this little activity after each battery of tests. I start to hear some really encouraging talk around the room.

"Can you help me with telling time? Your card says you are good at time..."

"Hey! I met my goal from last time and got better at subtracting!"

"I think I'm going to play the money game at center time because counting coins is really hard for me."

And just like that, I think that maybe I have found a silver lining to all this testing. Until...

At our next mandatory math meeting (read: torture session), The Bacon Hunter (yes, she's baaack!) notices the goal cards taped to my friends' desks. She asks about them. And in the spirit of my renewed optimism, I tell her my newfound plan and its surprising results. During my entire spiel no emotion registers on her face at all. Occasionally she glances at the cards taped to the desks around her, but I can't tell if she's even interested. Perhaps if they were bacon scented?

Then, lo and behold a few weeks later, all the lower grade teachers receive the following email.

Teachers,

Recently, a new strategy occurred to me that will be implemented across the lower grades. Effective immediately, each teacher is to assist students in creating personal goals for their learning in math. After giving our instruction a great deal of thought, I have decided that this will push our students to take more ownership of their own learning. Students are to fill out the attached rubric (which I have created) and write their goal in the upper left-hand corner. Please note it is to be written in the upper left-hand corner and nowhere else on the page. This is essential. Once each child determines a goal, these rubrics are to be filed with your math assessments. Remember, I can ask to see these materials at any time, so please follow through with this new initiative.

The Bacon Hunter

I have *got* to stop checking my email! Um, is she freaking kidding me? Several thoughts race through my brain simultaneously.

First of all, *she* thought of this new strategy? It just occurred to *her*? Like she was sitting on the subway or something when genius struck her? Or, wait, maybe she was sitting in *my classroom*…Not that I need to have the credit, but puh-lease. So just because something worked for *me* in *my classroom* with *my students*, we can assume that it will work for everyone? What makes her think that other teachers don't have their own way of doing the same thing? Why do we always have to do things exactly the same way? Do we want teachers or circus monkeys?

Second, the kids are supposed to write down their goals, and then the teacher files them away out of sight? (Don't get me started on that upper left-hand corner bit.) Ah yes, I can hear it now…children saying things such as, "Approximately two weeks ago, I wrote that I wanted to get better at counting coins…I better get on that."

And finally, how the hell does she still have a job? Better yet, how is it that I haven't just punched her in the face yet?

Well, I flat out refuse to change my system. It works in my classroom. And I'm tenured, so suck on that, Bacon Hunter. It will be a nice break for your teeth.

I'M GUESSING THAT you've been able to pick up on my anger. After all, I've never been one to feel or do anything subtly...just ask Mr. Mimi.

You can imagine what first went through my head when The Weave popped into my room on Friday morning to hang for our morning meeting. (Well, you're going to need to imagine it, because even I wouldn't have the *cajónes* to put that kind of foul language into print.)

At the end of the day, I rushed through the office in an attempt to avoid the bulletlike demands of our barking secretary and found a note from The Weave in my mailbox.

I read the note on the way back up to my classroom. I was so shocked by what it said, that I almost walked straight into my locked classroom door.

She gave me a compliment.

Wait! Not *one* compliment, *many* compliments. About my lesson, its tone, my classroom, and my interactions with the children. Hold on, let me read this again, that can't be right. She's talking about my *actual teaching*.

But it is, I have received an actual compliment. I feel strange, and unsure of how to take this new sort of interaction. Should I trust it? Is it a trick? Is her note missing a page filled with other scathing remarks?

Yes, there is more. There's feedback. Actual constructive commentary that might help me improve my work with kids.

Addicted to the odd display of positivity and promise, I quickly read her feedback. It read, "During your morning meeting, you reviewed some strategies for addition problems with your class. Your kids had great ideas. Perhaps you could chart those ideas and post them somewhere in your room. Better yet, maybe you could somehow credit each child with the strategy they shared. Here's an example." And she sketches what this chart might look like, followed by a big smiley face.

Great idea, right?

It would have been, if she hadn't been sitting in front of the *exact same chart* as she was observing our morning routine. Yeah, we made one. And displayed it. And she sat right in front of it. Seriously, like two feet away (sigh).

Her heart was in the right place, I guess. Now as for her keen powers of observation, we'll have to save those for another day. Baby steps, people.

AND THEN, LIKE always, one of my little friends manages to pull me back into what is really important (read: off the ledge).

Muppet is one of my sweetest little boys. He is super-mini, has giant brown eyes and crazy curly hair. He actually looks an awful lot like a Dr. Seuss or Jim Henson character, hence the nickname. Muppet is helpful, kind to others, and tries very hard in class. He can also be a huge space cadet. Sadly, he struggles more than some of my other students.

After discovering that many second graders at our school could not consistently or accurately name their continent, country, or state, my Super Colleagues and I added some much needed instruction to our social studies curriculum. We spent a series of weeks locating ourselves on the map and were wrapping up our teaching with a quick quiz, just to see how everyone was doing.

One of the items on our little quiz asked children to name the directions on a compass rose. At the time, we thought we were lobbing up an easy question for kids to knock out of the park. They had learned about north, south, east, and west in first grade and we had just spent a great deal of time reviewing and using these directions. Evidently, it was not enough time. When asked to *name* the four directions, Muppet wrote (no joke): Frank, Bobby, Sam, and Jack.

I almost inhaled my coffee when I read that one. Thank you, Muppet. Clearly we have to do some more work with the compass, but thank you.

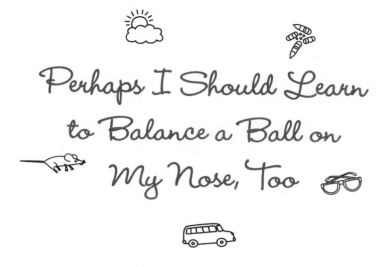

Perhaps I Should Learn to Balance a Ball on My Nose, Too

I FIND TEACHING TO be one big balancing act. I balance the needs of my low students with those of my high students. I balance more direct teaching with open-ended projects. I balance hour after hour of worthless meetings with actual productive planning time with my Super Colleagues. Seriously, I sometimes feel as if I am one balancing act short of putting a ball on my nose.

Perhaps the biggest balancing act for me is balancing my professional life with my personal life. You know how some children think that their teachers live at school? Well, there are also a lot of pompous jerks out there who believe that all teachers skip out of the building as soon as the children leave and spend their summers in a haze of free time. I mean, that's why we became teachers right, for the summers off? I for one got into teaching because I am lazy. When I was in college, I said to myself, "Self, to what can you dedicate your life of slovenly ways? Ooooh! I know! I'll be a teacher!" If you can't yet pick up on my heavy use of sarcasm, then I am afraid that you have zero sense of humor.

Most of the time, I fail miserably at this personal/professional balancing act. I *never* leave school with the kids, instead spending sometimes two or three hours in my classroom dealing with piles of paperwork and plans for the next few days. And, I *always* think about my little friends once I am at home again. It's gotten to the point that Mr. Mimi is often afraid to ask about my day because he is all too familiar with the usual tirade of complaints and endless tangents that quickly turn a two-minute answer into a thirty-minute monologue.

MR. MIMI: (pouring us each a glass of wine) "How was your day, sweetheart?"

ME: "Oh my God! It was so crazy! You will never believe what The Bacon Hunter said to me…"

MR. MIMI: (after 20 minutes of intense listening) "Wow. That sounds tough."

ME: "And then…we were right in the middle of writing when…"

MR. MIMI: (pouring himself another glass of wine) "Mmmm-hmmmm."

ME: "Oh! And did I tell you about Curly? I don't know what I would do without that kid. I was reading a story at the rug and he…"

MR. MIMI: (searching for the wine opener so that he can uncork another bottle) "I see."

I am completely unable to leave school at school. In fact, school totally rules my world and has taken over my life.

Thank goodness I am a huge nerd. Huge. Unfortunately, my nerdiness goes *way* back into my childhood and manifested itself both physically and mentally. When I was in junior high, I actually resembled Screech from *Saved by the Bell*. Really. I wouldn't make that up, because it is horrifying. And it is only recently that I have decided to embrace my former heinousness rather than be humiliated when it rears its ugly, frizzy head in pictures and old home movies. In addition to my personal hair travesty, I sported giant red glasses. Just to give you a nice visual, think Sally Jessy Raphael. For real. I don't care what my mother says, they were not cute. And on the mental front, I have always harbored a love for school. I think that's how I wound up still taking classes at the age of thirty. A little secret: I have taken only one year away from school since I was four years old. Yep, that's right, I went straight from high school to college, from college to a master's program, and after one year away from stuffy classrooms and incessant PowerPoint presentations, I found myself in a doctoral program, blissfully writing papers and plowing my way through text. (Okay, it hasn't always been that blissful. There have definitely been overwhelming periods of crying, low self-esteem, and intense procrastination followed by soul-crushing stress...wait, what am I doing to myself?)

To use an overly saccharine and worn-out phrase, I am going to go ahead and declare myself a lifelong learner. While I never intended for 90 percent of my personal and professional lives to revolve around the school experience, teaching has become somewhat of an addiction. Along with high heels, good coffee, and expensive trips to Barnes & Noble. Oh, maybe we should add all things cheese to that list, too, in the name of being thorough.

As you already know, I love my planner. And Post-it notes. I feel truly in my element when sitting with my Super Colleagues as we create new units of study and discover new read alouds. My heart pounds with excitement when we have one of those rare professional development sessions that results in a whole new outlook on math, and I walk away with a million ideas to implement into my classroom. Although I've never admitted it to anyone before, I also get a little teary eyed during those lessons when my friends are totally jazzed by what we are learning. And while I shun crying in public, I allow myself this little indulgence because it is truly a beautiful thing to be a part of that energy. Sometimes, they will say something during a class conversation that makes me want to scream and hug them because in that moment I realize that they really *are* listening and making progress.

Last week I was helping Bubbles with some math privately at her desk. In a moment of clarity, she looked at me and exclaimed, "Wait! Division is the opposite of multiplication just like subtraction is the opposite of addition!"

Again, I die.

When I am genuinely excited about what we are doing, it is a breeze to get the kids all worked up, too.

ME: "You guys, I am so excited! I have the coolest game to share with you. I used to play this game when I was little. I had a friend who lived next door..."

KIDS: (eyes wide, practically salivating as I continue to explain how to play marbles)

ME: "See this picture? That's me and my friend."

KIDS: (laughing) "You look funny!"

ME: (laughing) "I know, right? We're going to play that game right now and I want you to think about what makes the marbles move when they get stuck in the middle."

And before you know it, my little friends have played marbles and, in their own way, basically articulated Newton's first law of motion. Hot, right?

Now if you're wondering, these fabulously brilliant lessons were not pulled from a dusty old manual. They also weren't prepackaged into some "idiot-proof" curriculum, because, contrary to much public belief, teachers are not idiots. These ideas are the direct result of time spent with my Super Colleagues and hours of preparation.

And now, I will climb upon my soapbox and begin my diatribe on scripted curriculum. Have a seat, grab a cocktail...I can wait.

Scripted curriculum is bullshit.

Gosh, that felt good to say out loud. Let me say it again. Scripted curriculum is bullshit.

The most offensive aspect of these scripted curriculums is the evil companies that market them as small miracles in a box. As if a teacher simply needs to go through the motions laid out in painful detail in the manual and voilà! The children have learned. Clearly, these morons have never been in a classroom. Or they have confused teachers with trained circus animals, I don't know. One or the other. You pick.

The sad thing is, there are actually some good ideas buried deep down in these scripted programs. Some were even created with solid research beneath them. But, hello, talk about hero complex, people! Claiming that there is only *one* way to teach reading and *this is it*... Arguing that within these pages are the tools to teach every single child in every single imaginable context...tone it down, Jim Jones, I am not drinking that Kool-Aid.

Sadly, the Kool-Aid was forced upon me once, early in my career when I was too new to do anything about it. Picture it. Harlem, 2001. A young girl sets off into the world of education with nothing but a pair of high-heeled shoes on her feet and a master's degree in her hand. She stumbles upon a school in a neighborhood just gritty enough and is hired in a matter of days. Anxious to start her new life, she eagerly awaits her first professional development conference, which she is scheduled to attend during her first month as a Real Teacher.

The morning of that fateful day, she packs up her brand-new Teacher Bag and skips out the door. She observes the other Real Teachers around her, drinking in their habits, mannerisms, and ways of speaking. She watches as the professional development leader unpacks her bag, noting the very large owl puppet perched on the desk. Little does the girl know that she is about to endure a six-hour "training session" designed to prepare her to implement the most mind-numbing phonics curriculum known to man.

Friends, I was that young girl. And the professional development leader was a complete insult to educators everywhere. Oh, and a huge tool.

I learned that day that one of the key features of this program was speaking to the children via a puppet. Now, I may teach small children, and like them very much, but puppets? I don't do puppets. But I thought, hey, no big deal, I just won't use the puppet. I mean, there's no connection between using a puppet and a child's ability to learn the sounds of the alphabet, right?

Um, wrong. Severely wrong. This program was so complete in its brainwashing of both students and teachers that it included scripted portions for the teacher to read verbatim (both as herself and as the puppet). Even the praise for a correct answer was scripted; you couldn't spice it up with your own little flavor. Oh, and the puppet? Mandatory.

I know what you're probably thinking. Just lock the puppet deep in your mouse-poo–filled closet and forget about it. Right? Wrong. Because we were told that people with clipboards would be coming around and checking up on us. (I know, again with the clipboards!) And they wanted to see the owl. I guess breezing by my classroom and seeing me hoot like a crazy person was good enough for them. Check! There must be good learning going on in *that* classroom. Listen to her hoot!

As I learned during those two days, sticking my hand up an owl's ass was absolutely essential to the teaching of phonics. I never quite saw the logic. The presenter lost me completely when she spoke to us, a group of 25 grown women, via the puppet.

HER: (hooting) "Whooooo can tell me the sound short 'a' makes?"

ME: "Seriously?"

HER: (more hooting) "Seriously! Role-playing is very effective in the training of teachers."

ME: "Training? You are *training* us? Like we're seals?"

HER: (enthusiastic hooting) "Yooou got it!"

ME: "And I get to be the kid in this little scenario?"

HER: "You got it!" (vigorous flapping of owl wings)

ME: "Then can I go to the bathroom?"

She then went on to tell us that this curriculum was so "foolproof" (I assume that teachers are the fools she was proofing against), that it could be taught in a coma. A coma? That's right, I said a coma. Evidently, all we need to do is pull out the card for that day, collect the necessary supplies, and do what it says on the card. In my mind, this makes me the card's bitch. But maybe I'm missing something; after all, I'm the fool in this scenario. And if these magical cards really do exist, where's the one for How to Deal with People Who Insult My Intelligence?

Teach in a coma? Is this what she thinks will win us over? Perhaps she imagined us saying, "A coma? Fabulous! Get me that curriculum *now!*" I look around for similarly incredulous looks, but no one seems to be bothered by what I think she is so clearly implying: Teachers want the easy way out, because we can't do it ourselves. (I mean, we are fools, right? Those who can't do, teach?)

My hand shoots up and my fellow Super Colleagues glance at me nervously. They already know me all too well.

HER: "Yes, you in the fabulous shoes."

ME: (thinking, "That's right, sister, they are fabulous.")
"Um, so I'm going to like using this program because I don't have to do any thinking?"

HER: "That's right, sweetheart." (She makes the owl nod along with her. Yeah, she's still holding the freaking owl.)

ME: (Did she just call me sweetheart? I think I just saw my Super Colleagues cringe.) "Um, okay. So, you did all the thinking for me? That's amazing. Without ever meeting my class or knowing what their needs are?"

HER: "You are sassy! Yes, this program is guaranteed to work for every child. We know what they need. You can just relax." (At this point the Owl Lady makes a triumphant hooting noise.)

ME: "Relax and fall into a coma?"

I stopped talking to The Owl Lady at this point because I was afraid that I may leap over the table and wring her neck. Or do something very wrong to her beloved owl puppet. I am horrified that she actually thinks that there is something that will work for *every* child…and that teachers just want to stop thinking.

Then I realize that these types of programs are created for teachers like The Fanny Pack, who really aren't capable of a whole lot more. Personally, I'm not comfortable setting the bar quite so low for teachers.

Because I am also a doctoral student at a nearby fancy-pants university, my head is brimming with all sorts of theories and studies I prepared for class that week. And so I used my knowledge for good instead of evil (depending on how you look at it) and reached for my Evaluation of the Program. I then spent the next hour writing a scathing review of the presentation, complete with a reference section.

I think some of my Real Teacher self died that day.

SINCE THEN, I have learned a thing or two about balancing what I think is the right thing to do in my classroom with what everyone else says I should be doing. And by "everyone else," I mean all sorts of people who, for some unknown reason, get to have an opinion about what goes on in schools, regardless of the fact that they neither work in schools themselves nor have any experience as an educator. Discuss.

Fortunately for me, The Visionary is obsessed with professional development (please don't say the word "training" to me again!) so I am able to balance the good with the bad. After many, many bad sessions, in which I resorted to frantic list making as a method of calming my frayed nerves (yes, list making calms me down: I already told you I am a giant nerd), The Visionary sent me a gift in the form of the most amazingly relevant, intelligent, and positive outside math staff developer ever.

Enter my Teacher Crush.

Just to clarify: A Teacher Crush is not like a I Think You're Hot Crush…no, no, no. It's much more nerdy than that. (Besides, I have a fabulously gorgeous husband who is the love of my life…I need not look any further in that department.) It's more like a crush on someone who is just so damn brilliant and good at their job. An inspirational teacher who just has this way of looking at things that you want to emulate. This person doesn't even really need to be a man, just someone fabulously smart. But it doesn't hurt that he's a man. Teaching in an elementary school can just be sad sometimes. It's really just a building brimming with women. Women and thanklessness.

It is like a ray of sunshine when in walks my Teacher Crush, full of praise and amazing constructive ideas.

ME: "Hi, how are you? Thanks for coming to my room today."

HIM: "I loved your mini-lesson. It was short and to the point and really got them started."

ME: (big, goofy smile)

HIM: "And the children seem really engaged."

ME: (bigger, goofier smile)

HIM: "I really like how independent the children seem in the room. It's a great space. But I have a couple of things you might want to try..."

I stared at my Teacher Crush with wide eyes, soaking in all the praise and constructive criticism. (Maybe insert the occasional eyelash bat...old habits die hard, people.)

How sad am I? You think teachers need a little more encouragement? Or positive reinforcement? Kids aren't the only ones who need a sticker every once in awhile.

My Teacher Crush left me a love note on that day. Not a love note filled with illicit images or whispered promises, but a love note filled with kind words about my work in the classroom and interesting ideas for me to try. His thoughtful words of encouragement and new strategies provided a much-needed balance to The Bacon Hunter's sleepy-eyed attempts at just paying attention.

And like a pathetic love-starved teenager, I taped this love note to the inside of my closet, for those lonelier days when The Bacon Hunter rains on my educational parade.

RECENTLY, THE BALANCE between professional development meetings and time in the classroom has been *way* out of whack. The Visionary has erred on the side of overdeveloping us, and we are in meetings every day of the week. I mean, it's the middle of January, I have a million things left to teach, and the end of the year is looming large, but I am constantly out of a classroom getting...developed (for lack of a better word). Which means my friends are left with a substitute, and I am left scribbling down hour after hour of useless sub plans, while pushing the activities I would like to do off for another week. I wish someone had told me (when I was a starry-eyed teenager sitting in my Intro to Education class) that the teacher's schedule takes absolute last priority to every other imaginable schedule in the school building. Randomly scheduled field trips are a priority. Concerts are a priority. Staff development meetings are a priority. The Bacon Hunter's incessant batteries of tests are a priority. After all these priorities, I am left with the odds and ends of the week and must desperately cobble together something worthwhile. (So you can see where I am left with the impression of my relative place on the food chain?)

But you see, the balance of how often I am in the

classroom rocking it out, and how often I am out of the classroom in meeting after meeting, is a crucial one. When this balance gets thrown off, it is a slippery slope into Wild and Crazy Town.

A little recap of my unbalanced week.

Scene 1: Monday morning. My friends are gathered on the carpet in a circle. We have just said good morning to one another.

ME: Okay guys. I have another meeting today.

THEM: Awwwww…

ME: (Love it! Of course you miss me when I'm gone!) I know, I know. I'd rather be here with you, too, but I'll see you again after lunch. And I know you'll be super stars while I'm out of the room.

THEM: (Vigorous nodding.)

Scene 2: Tuesday morning. My friends are gathered on the carpet in a circle. We have just said *buenos días* to one another.

ME: All right. So after Readers' Workshop, I've got to go to another meeting until lunch, but I'll be back.

THEM: What? Huh? *Another* meeting?

ME: Sorry, friends. But I'll be back in the afternoon. You'll have a great morning with the substitute teacher.

THEM: Sure. (Some nodding, a few thumbs-up.)

Scene 3: Wednesday morning. My friends are gathered on the carpet in the circle. We have just said *bonjour* to one another.

ME: So, I have a meeting today after lunch.

THEM: *Another meeting?!* (They shoot each other incredulous glances.)

ME: Yeah, another meeting. Today I'm going to go learn some fabulous new art we can do together.

THEM: (sighs) Okaaaay.

ME: And I know you'll do your best for the substitute.

THEM: (Furtive, sneaky glances are exchanged.)

ME: Right?

THEM: (Offhandedly...distracted, as if they are plotting something...) Yeah.

ME: I have prizes for people who listen...

Yes, I have resorted to bribery. Sadly, it was too little too late. Stickers are no longer enough to quell their rage at having their teacher taken away. My friends, who were troopers on Monday and Tuesday, have decided on Wednesday to rebel against the system that is robbing them of their teacher day after day. Translation: They are bat-shit crazy when the substitute is in the room with them.

I return from my art meeting feeling fairly Zen. After all, I've been experimenting with paint and exchanging ideas with my Super Colleagues for the last hour and a half. My friends on the other hand are looking very guilty as I walk into the room. A hush fills the air as I step inside and several children are frozen in mid bad choice. The substitute looks worse for wear and hands me a list of children with the heading Bad. It doesn't look good.

With that in mind, imagine how I felt when I had finally settled my friends into a very productive Writer's Workshop period and one of my girls showed me the little secret message that was left on her folder.

In fairly large letters it says "Foke you."

"Foke you"? Yeah, it means what you think.

We had to leave for gym in a few minutes so I kept it private at first. But I had several immediate thoughts as I brought my friends downstairs to the cafeteria.

Thought #1

Whoever it was spelled the "F word" with a sneaky "e"! I mean, do you hear the long "o" sound in the F word, friends? No, you do not. And we have been talking about long and short vowels for the last few weeks. I am seriously more disappointed in their vowel choices than I am in their defacing of classroom property...how screwed up is that?

Thought #2

I am so annoyed that I have to deal with this afternoon because I know it is all a result of them being stuck with a sub. I hate those moments when I have to choose the battle and deal...

Thought #3

Maybe I can relish the gnarly guilt trip I'm about to lay on them...hmmm...this could get juicy.

Thought #4

You know what? Foke you, too. Those folders were expensive and took me forever to label.

So they get back from gym and we have an emergency class meeting. I lay it on thick. It was genius. The Tony people totally should have been there. It went a little something like this:

ME: (blah blah blah, this is what happened, I am so disappointed, blah blah blah...). "I know who did this (I totally don't). And I could just punish that person. But I want them to learn something about responsibility. We are all responsible for making this classroom a place we all look forward to coming to. Today someone decided not to hold up their end of the deal and did not take care of us. I'm going to give everyone a slip of paper. If you have a clear heart and conscience, you can just write me a quick hello on your paper. If you have a sad heart and know you need to be a responsible citizen of our class, you can privately tell me what you've done."

No one fessed up. *Foke!*

It was worth a try. I'm not done yet, either. A note went home to all the parents and I'm expecting a tearful confession in the a.m.

Hopefully this is the last time my mystery friend will foke around in class!

(Sigh) Sometimes I *so* don't feel like being the adult.

IRACULOUSLY, ON THURSDAY, I didn't have to go to any meetings. Thank goodness, because I think my little friends would have lost their minds if I made that announcement again this week. We should be able to have a normal day, which is a relief, because I have not been able to do any actual teaching yet this week, what with all the professional development. I wonder when The Visionary thinks we're going to *try* all the stuff we learn if we are never actually in our classrooms…but that is a discussion for another day.

We are sitting in a circle on the rug and have just greeted one another with a hearty *"Jambo!"* when I receive a phone call on my classroom phone.

ME: (picking up the phone) "Hello?"

THE WEAVE: "Can you send down Curly?"

ME: "Is there a problem? We were just about to start Readers' Workshop…"

THE WEAVE: "Just send him down. I'll explain later."

Evidently keeping me in the loop is her last priority. Right next to my schedule. Maybe I'm not going to get my normal day after all. I send Curly downstairs and try to get on with the day.

Later, I am officially in the know. And what I know is three days with a substitute equals a week's worth of drama. Apparently, Curly patted another little girl's bottom during a read aloud when I was out of the room at a meeting. We'll call this little girl The Victim. The Victim says nothing to the substitute and Curly just went on with his day...clearly the guilt was easy to overcome.

So, The Victim then goes home and tells her parents. The Victim's parents come in to demand a meeting and throw around words like "sexual harassment." A bit much in my opinion but I'm just going to go with it...I don't mess around with this whole "privates" business.

Let's fast-forward to the big powwow, shall we?

Scene: The Weave's office.

Characters: myself, The Weave, The Victim and her parents, Curly and his parents.

We are just about to wrap up what I thought to be a very successful little talk on keeping your hands to yourself.

ME: "So what have you learned, Curly?"

CURLY: "I shouldn't touch anyone during school...especially in their 'privates.'" (Insert angelic look and some eyelash fluttering here.)

ME: "The Victim? What did you learn?"

THE VICTIM: "I learned that I have to tell the teacher when something makes me feel uncomfortable. It's okay to ask for a private conversation, especially when it's about my 'privates.'" (Imagine her young feminist self blossoming during this brief speech...girl power, honey!)

ME: "Super."

THE WEAVE: "I'm so proud of you both. I'm glad you learned your lesson, Curly. Remember, you have a lifetime of touching other girls' privates...you don't need to start now."

Whoah! Let me say that again...a little bit louder now...

And I quote: "YOU HAVE A LIFETIME OF TOUCHING OTHER GIRLS' PRIVATES!"

Do you even *see* the parents sitting in your office? They are not wearing camouflage. What are you thinking?

Glad you get double my pay. You sure earned that extra cash today.

AND NOW (you guessed it!), it's time for yet another heart-warming moment from the main office:

Finally, it was Friday and the longest week I can

remember having was almost over. I stopped by the office to check my mail and see if my copies had been made. If only so much of my professional life didn't revolve around mail and copies...

There was a huge pile of copies shoved lovingly into my box along with a ton of assorted memos. I pulled the crumpled mass out of my mailbox and headed upstairs. Once in my classroom, I sorted through the daunting pile. I had my copies, a notice about picture day, a memo to go home to parents, and...wait a minute, what's this?

I pull a brightly colored postcard out of the mangled heap. It is an invitation to a sex toy party, like one of those Tupperware parties but with more sex toys and fewer crudités.

Oh my.

One of the office workers came running into my room at that moment.

"Um, I think some of my stuff got mixed in with your copies," she said, her face bright red.

"You mean this?"

"Yeah. Sorry! I just thought it would be easier to use the school copier instead of going to Staples and paying for it. Everyone there is so rude."

So I'm not the only one who thinks so! I thought. "Of course. Totally. Here you go."

"Thanks. I need to get these out. Sorry again. Please don't say anything."

"Of course not," I say, thinking that maybe I have found the key to getting copies done correctly and on time. Hey, I'm not above blackmail.

And, in a strange way, her mistake made me feel better about myself. Not that I want to host a party for sex toys, but it helped me to realize that I'm not the only one struggling with the whole personal/professional balance thing.

Teacher, Interrupted

WE WERE HAVING a particularly productive week. It was one of those weeks that makes me feel like a good teacher and reminds me why I teach in the first place. I brought my A-game, they brought their A-game. It's rare when the stars align so perfectly like that, but when it does happen, it's a beautiful thing. Luckily it happens every time I think I'm about to run screaming from the building and keeps me coming back for more.

Last week, I had my friends working in groups to design a very basic relief map of the United States. Bubbles was deeply involved with her group, debating the uses of black beans versus red string to represent our country's borders. After much heated conversation, a verdict was reached and Bubbles busily set to work, glue bottle in hand. As I passed by, she looked up and said, "Look, Mrs. Mimi, I'm learning!"

I die.

While I shun crying in public, I am not ashamed to say that I got a tear or two in my eye. I gave Bubbles the biggest hug and said, "Thank you, sweetheart."

So you can imagine my frustration when our academic stride was broken by the incessant ringing of the classroom phone.

Ring!

ME: "Hello?"

ANGRY VOICE: "Your copies are ready. Come and get them."

ME: "But I'm in the middle of…"

ANGRY VOICE: "Now."

ME: "…teaching."

Ring!

ME: "Hello?"

ANGRY VOICE: "You got Little Girl in your class?!"

ME: "Sorry, wrong…(phone slams down) classroom. Hello?"

Ring!

ME: "Yes?"

ANGRY VOICE: "I'm still waiting for you to pick up your copies. It's been fifteen minutes."

ME: "But I'm still in the middle of teaching."

Phone slams down.

I wonder why the voice on the other end of the phone is always so angry. It's never the case that the voice begins as pleasant and gets progressively angry during our phone calls, especially since the phone calls usually last all of ten irritable seconds. I mean, is it really necessary to go from zero to pissed in ten seconds? If you're so angry and impatient, why do you want to spend your day with children? Shouldn't you be spending your days with a bunch of counselors...perhaps in some sort of anger-management program?? I'm just sayin'...

I think it's safe to say at this point that I officially hate the phone. I entertain the idea of taking it off the hook and feigning innocence when I get caught, but I never manage to have the balls to actually pull the trigger. In the back of my mind I worry that the moment I do take the phone off the hook will be the same moment, and the *only* moment, someone truly needs to reach my classroom with some horrid emergency (sigh).

In addition to phone interruptions, we also have the

face-to-face interruptions. You know, when someone storms into the classroom making enough noise to ensure that the *entire* class is no longer paying attention and then asks you a completely worthless question that could have been handled in an email or, better yet, *after school*?

INTERRUPTER #1: (Slamming door behind them.) "Here are the letters that need to go home tonight."

INTERRUPTER #2: (Flinging door open so that it bangs into the wall. Stops and stares at me standing in front of 20 sets of expectant eyeballs.) "Are you busy?"

INTERRUPTER #3: (Dropping a giant set of photocopies onto a student's desk while said student is actually *at* the desk, attempting to work.) "Here are your copies!"

One particularly frustrating morning, we were just a few minutes into our day, and I was (gasp!) working with my students when three big, loud, strange plumbers walked into the classroom without knocking, making eye contact, or asking. They sauntered to the back of my classroom. They proceeded to turn the faucets on and off and use what we in the business refer to as "outside voices." Clearly, my friends' attention was riveted on these intruders (rather than on our shared story). We all watched and listened as one of them answered his cell phone and began to have what was clearly a personal conversation. Seriously.

Knowing it is wise to choose my battles, I told the few friends who were desperately trying to maintain focus to just go ahead, turn around, and watch. Upon noticing all the little eyes staring holes through his back, the most offensive offender turned and said, "Lady, I'm just trying to do my job."

Yes, me too, my man, me too.

After lunch, the same three men returned to my classroom (again, without knocking, making eye contact, or asking) to change a lightbulb, which necessitated them standing on a desk. While a child was working. At the desk.

It was at this point that I started chanting, "I love my job, I love my job, I love my job" in my head.

As we were packing up to go home (finally, the end of this ridiculous day was in sight!), our end-of-the-day routine is rudely interrupted, yet again, by the flippin' phone. Relinquishing my tenuous hold on their behavior, I reluctantly went to answer the phone. The security guard at the front desk demanded that I send down one of my friends packed up to go home.

"But we're leaving in seven minutes," I said.

"I don't care if you're on the way out the door; her mother doesn't want to wait," replied my not-so-polite co-worker.

"This is ridiculous, we're in the middle of packing up. She isn't ready. We'll be down in five."

"Her mother says she wants her daughter now. She's sick of waiting for *you* to be ready."

Deep breaths. I love my job, I love my job, I love my job?

I bring my friends downstairs, say good-bye, and head to the office to check my mail, thinking the worst is behind me. As I enter the office, a familiar bark comes my way.

"Mrs. Mimi!" barks our secretary.

"Yes?"

"Are you going to pick up your pay stub or do I have to send you a personal invitation?"

"Excuse me?"

"Your pay stub. Duh! It's been ready since one and you still haven't picked it up."

(Did she just say "Duh" to me?) "Um, well, I've been teaching since one. So, no, I haven't picked it up yet."

"Then why you just standing there? You think I gots all day?"

No, I think you "gots" some major issues with simple grammar and a huge attitude.

*U*NFORTUNATELY, the interruptions don't stop there. Oh no! The wastes of our learning time are numerous and unending. You see, there are also officially sanctioned wastes of time. And by sanctioned wastes of time, I mean people who are supposed to push into my classroom to support student learning. It sounds like a good idea in theory. But in practice, this type of "support" is rarely, well, supportive. Let me give you an example. We have certain teachers who are supposed to help out my English Language Learners during our reading time. Ideally, this teacher should listen to the lesson for the day and then meet with children individually or in a small group to support their language acquisition as well as provide them with specific strategies for advancing their reading ability. Instead, the individual assigned to my classroom, otherwise known as The Fanny Pack, evidently prefers to take up precious space, not listen, and leave empty water bottles strewn around the room.

Now, I know there are many of you out there who are currently pushing into classrooms and adding a tremendous amount of value. Maybe it's Newton's Law or something but for every one of you hard workers out there, there is an equal and opposite teacher. I think their mother ship might be my school.

I was in the middle of a brief reading lesson when I realized that I wasn't the only one merely tolerating The Fanny Pack's existence. Chubby Cheeks, perhaps one of the roundest, sweetest, and most hardworking children I have ever taught, clearly has trouble being polite, too. You see, Chubby Cheeks was sitting at the back of the rug, dutifully listening because he is fabulous. The Fanny Pack was sitting in a chair right next to Chubby Cheeks, who, incidentally, is a child she "works" with on a regular basis. Logic would dictate that she sat near him intentionally, but after working with her for many years, I know that this is simply a coincidence. Miracle of miracles, she realizes that Chubby Cheeks is right there and decides to all of a sudden do something and "work" with him. Mind you, I am totally still talking to the class, so yes, she gets some points for feigning work, but then she just loses those points again by talking when I'm talking. Anyhow, she leans over to talk to Chubby Cheeks and I notice that Chubby Cheeks starts leaning in the opposite direction to get away from her, all while never taking his eyes off me. She leans, he leans. I keep talking as I watch Chubby Cheeks inching away slowly, tipping further and further to the left as she moves closer and closer. And then, *bam*!

He falls all the way over and crashes into the child sitting next to him.

As Chubby Cheeks brings himself to a sitting position and I send everyone back to their seats to begin writing, I wonder how The Visionary allows this waste of space to waste so much space year after year. It's no secret that she is contributing absolutely nothing to our students' learning. So how has she not been fired? She's tenured, that's how. I just don't get tenure. Maybe it's because I'm relatively new, but from my perspective it seems that many (too many) are using their tenured status to relieve them from any actual work responsibility. Personally, I think it is absolutely offensive that we tolerate these individuals in our line of work. They make the rest of us look bad. How did these people even get tenure in the first place? Why is our school not weeding these people out *before* they are tenured if we know tenure is so freaking easy to get? In a sense, all you have to do is show up to work and not hit a kid and presto! You're tenured in three years. How is it even considered a professional achievement if everyone just gets it? I know it's about job protection and all that, but if you ask me, the best type of job protection is actually *doing your job well*. Clearly I think the system is broken and I'm not sure why we don't fix it.

Some people feel the need to compare schools to businesses and advocate for a "business model" for education.

Without going into my horrified tirade as to why this line of thinking is atrocious, let's just run with that popular little analogy for a moment, since it seems to be a fan favorite. Mr. Mimi is a business guy. He does business-y things in a business suit (and looks very cute, I might add!). Mr. Mimi has worked with a guy who clearly violated some of the systems put in place in order for his line of business to run smoothly and productively. This person got fired. Period. After taking advantage of the system, the business-y powers-that-be tanked him. So that begs the question, if we are so in love with a business model of education, why aren't we kicking butt and taking names when it comes to those who are so clearly taking advantage of the tenure system?

And if we're going to go that far in our thinking, how did this woman even get to be a teacher in the first place? Was she ever any good? On my more generous days, I think that maybe many, many years ago in a galaxy far, far away she *was* a good teacher. Perhaps, over the years, she has been crippled by a system that is more and more obsessed with scripted, mind-numbing curriculum that totally eradicates the need for teachers to think on their own. Seriously, there are all sorts of people working in schools who have been drinking the Kool-Aid when it comes to these "scientifically proven" programs. In my first year of teaching, I had to teach such a program and was told that if I simply made sure I made it through all the lessons, my children would learn to read. But maybe The Fanny Pack bought it, and she's still waiting for someone to hand her a manual and tell her what to do. So maybe she's not taking advantage of the system, maybe the system took advantage of her, and as a result, totally robbed her of any ability to think for herself. Fortunately, at our school, we've evolved way past that, sister. Despite all my complaining, really amazing things are happening for children: teachers are creating authentic and engaging learning opportunities (that don't come from a manual) left and right. It's time to put down that fanny pack and flex those (incredibly weak) teacher muscles, girlfriend!

But as I step off my soapbox and back into reality, I am fed up with interruptions and sensing my professional façade about to crack in front of all my little friends, I decided to turn my frown upside down and seize the teachable moment. Because in my world, constant interruptions plus curricular connections times a teacher with an attitude equals a brilliant teachable moment.

Let me explain. Earlier in the week, we had been reviewing how to make and read tally marks. We had also been doing a bit of graphing. So I thought to myself, "Self, why not have your friends create a tally-mark chart that tracks all the interruptions to our classroom over one week?"

Game on. After The Fanny Pack left, we had a brief

discussion about what constituted a legitimate interruption and what was just a waste of our time. (I exercised my professionalism by *not* including a tirade on the uselessness of many push-in teachers at our school...hey, it's the least I could do.) Then we posted our chart in a corner of the classroom. Our investigation had officially begun. Each day that week we feverishly tally marked, finding a total at the end of each day. By the end of that week we were practically blown away by our findings: We had been interrupted a grand total of 47 times in five days! (If you aren't shocked right now, go back, re-read these last few paragraphs, and fake it for me, because it is shocking!)

To tie our experience together, we composed a group letter to our principal, explaining our methodology. And as I walked out of the building that Friday afternoon, I casually popped both our letter and the tally-mark chart into my principal's mailbox.

Deep down, I knew that nothing would come of our little data-collection experience. I could already picture The Visionary pulling our work out of his mailbox, briefly scanning the letter, and shaking his head. On my way home, I realized I had two choices. I could either spend the rest of the year fuming about these wastes of time masquerading as teachers or I could make peace with their existence.

As a therapeutic exercise, I took advantage of my 35-minute commute that afternoon and penned an open letter to some of the infamous Drains on Student Learning at my school. I thought that this was a more productive use of my time than stalking them in the hallways and punching them in the face. I will now share that letter with all of you. (You're welcome in advance.)

To Whom It May Concern:

Today I have decided to stop fooling myself into thinking that you might actually do your jobs and finally accept that many of you are as useful as a sack of hair. Sacks of hair that receive a biweekly paycheck for wasting children's time to be exact. Yes, at times I find your socially awkward ways charming and your ceaselessly creative antics designed to avoid any sort of actual work amusing. In fact, I think I should thank you for much of the material in my book. However, I have wasted too much time scripting the scathing remarks that I will never have the nerve to say to your face. I have wasted too much time seething about your constant inability to stick to a schedule, follow through with your job requirements, or make any significant impact on children. I have wasted too much time fantasizing about painting your office door yellow and posting a huge sign that reads Caution: Human Roadblocks to Student Learning Ahead.

I am going to be the bigger person and apologize to you (because I have realized that you will never apologize to me or my students for the precious hours of our time spent in your company that we will never get back). I apologize for all the times when I smirked at your obvious inability to grasp even the most basic classroom practices. I apologize for all the times when my pinched facial expression, tense shoulders, and curt replies clearly illustrated the intense irritation I experienced when speaking to you in any capacity. And finally, I apologize that I tried as hard as I did to include you in our daily routine. I thought you were anxious to help our most troubled learners make significant improvements. My mistake. It won't happen again.

Sincerely,

Mrs. Mimi

Now you might be saying to yourself, "What a hugely arrogant letter! Who does this Mrs. Mimi person think she is anyway? Some sort of teaching guru?"

And the answer is yes, I am a tad arrogant. But no, I am not a teaching guru. However, I am fairly positive that

I am much more qualified to stand in front of a group of small children and claim to advance their learning. Let me give you an example of a conversation that I had with The Fanny Pack that may illustrate exactly what we're dealing with here.

THE FANNY PACK: "I just don't understand." (Awkwardly long pause and some incoherent grunting.)

ME: (Speaking because I can't stand the weird silence.) "What don't you understand?"

THE FANNY PACK: "This new reading curriculum. We never used to do it this way."

ME: "You mean the one we've been using for the last three years?" (I know, I'm a bitch.)

THE FANNY PACK: "Yeah."

ME: "Oh, what part are you having trouble with?"

THE FANNY PACK: "All of it! (More grunting.) There are so many new terms to learn. It's too much. Like, what's a Read Aloud?"

ME: "Um, it's when you read a book…out loud."

THE FANNY PACK: "What? What? What is that?" (Now frantic.)

Me: "Gee, I'm not really sure how to break that down any other way. You know, when you get a picture book and read it out loud to the class?"

THE FANNY PACK: (incredulous tone) *"Picture* book? What?"

ME: "I have to go."

So, no, I am not a master teacher. Some days I am not even sure I am very good at my job. However, I do know that I bust my behind while others, like my friend The Fanny Pack, sit back and collect a paycheck.

But no matter what I think, the machine that is education keeps churning and like many things in schools, those little irritations will cycle right back to haunt me again. They might not look exactly the same and they may have a new snazzy name, but they are still disruptions at heart.

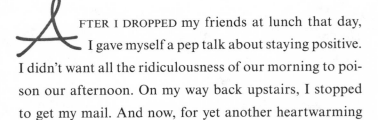

FTER I DROPPED my friends at lunch that day, I gave myself a pep talk about staying positive. I didn't want all the ridiculousness of our morning to poison our afternoon. On my way back upstairs, I stopped to get my mail. And now, for yet another heartwarming moment from the main office (a.k.a. experiences that chip away at my soul and eat positive attitudes alive):

The previous day, I put in a request for 100 copies of the second grade homework packet. It's my turn to create our homework for the month, so I needed a class set for each teacher. When I checked my mailbox that afternoon, I found 13 copies of the packet. Not only is this not enough for my class, it is nowhere near the 100 copies I asked for. So, I did some mental math and put in another request for 87 copies of the homework packet.

Earlier this morning, I stopped by my mailbox and pulled out 27 more copies of the homework. I slowly counted to ten, the way my grandmother did when she used to watch me after school, and did the math. I already had 13 copies, so 27 more made 40. I put in a request for 60 additional copies of the homework packet.

On the way back to my classroom, I found 33 copies of the homework packet in my mailbox. It was at this point that I called upon my deep yoga breathing to keep from slamming someone's face into the photocopier and making 100 copies. I calmly went to our photocopy person and asked if I could finish the copies myself. She said no, that I was not qualified to touch the photocopier.

Of course I'm not. Let's just say I am now holding on to my Positive Attitude like it is a life raft.

A T THIS POINT you should be familiar with my obsession with pee. Pee is another uncontrollable force that can also be extremely disruptive. I spend an unreasonable amount of time laying out what one might call Pee Policies at the beginning of the year, describing in detail when and how often children may use the bathroom, emergencies withstanding. I would like them to be able to monitor their own need to pee, going only at unintrusive times, yet realize that my desire might just be out of their reach. Despite my efforts, the issue of The Bathroom haunts me on and off throughout the year.

After lunch, we were in the middle of word study when one of my friends asked to go to the bathroom. Now usually I don't allow my friends to go to the bathroom when I am dispensing genius, but this friend looked particularly desperate and uncomfortable, so I let him go. Nobody wants the old puddle on the floor, especially me. We continued on with our word study game and at least 15 minutes go by when I start to wonder where the hell my friend is. I am mentally writing the scathing note home to his mother in my head when I hear the telltale slam of the boy's bathroom door.

He's coming. What am I going to do…hmmmm…how wicked do I feel? Those phone calls and photocopies really did put me in quite a mood…but none of my mood is the fault of my little friends.

I look over at the woman who "pushes in" to my classroom each day at this time. No, it's not The Fanny

Pack this time. It's little Ms. Know It All, a newer teacher who feels as if she has nothing to learn despite the fact that she's never taught before. Ms. Know It All is famous for talking in an inappropriately loud voice, even when the classroom teacher is talking, and generally undoing all of my good work by thoroughly confusing children who already struggle to begin with. Basically, I spend the 50 minutes a day either shooting Ms. Know It All sly dirty looks when she talks over me or muttering under my breath. Very professional, I know.

Anyway, I look over at Ms. Know It All and wonder if she will think I'm a bitch for laying into my friend about screwing around in the bathroom while the rest of the class is working. I am considering my options when (insert sound of screeching tires here) he walks in and everything stops.

He is literally covered from head to toe in his own shit. (Sorry, Mom, but no other word even comes close.) It has apparently run down his leg and it is oozing out of his shoes. It is all over his hands. And yes, boys and girls, there is shit on his face.

What did they serve for lunch?

I have to think fast! I can't let him sit down. I can't let the class start to laugh. And I certainly can't touch him.

For some reason, the whole class is silent. It's like time stopped. You think that a group of seven year olds would lose their minds with this recent development in our day. I mean, someone *covered in shit* has just walked into the room! What? I silently remind myself to thank them later.

ME: "Honey, are you okay?"

HIM: "Uh, I was trying to clean up."

ME: (to myself) *Clean up? Did your butt explode? How does that happen? And again, what did they serve for lunch?* (out loud) "Okay, sweetheart. It's okay."

HIM: "I don't feel good."

ME: "It's okay, honey. Uh, Ms. Know It All? Do you think you could walk him to the nurse?" (I'm still not sure why shit on your face qualifies you for the medical attention of the nurse, but then again that seems to be the place to send most things you don't want to deal with...although usually they come back with a cough drop and a completely illegible note. Seriously, you slice your finger open and that woman would give you a cough drop and send you back to class clutching a paper filled with hieroglyphics in your few remaining fingers.)

MS. KNOW IT ALL: "What?"

ME: (to myself of course) *Ha ha! That will teach you to talk when I'm talking! Sucka!* (out loud) "Thank you."

Somehow I manage to spin my friend around without touching him and go back to my lesson. He squishes out of the room and waits for Ms. Know It All. What a good boy. I watch as she reluctantly follows his brown trail out the door and down the hall.

No bad deed goes unpunished, though. I knew what I was doing when I asked Ms. Know It All to take our poo-covered friend to the nurse on that poo-filled day. I rationalized it by telling myself that there was no way I could leave the class unattended, but also took a bit too much pleasure in asking Ms. Know It All to do me that little favor.

I guess sometimes I like to think that after years of hard work and multiple advanced degrees that maybe, just maybe, my workplace is somewhere that welcomes dry-clean-only pants and doesn't insist on giving me hideous ailments such as the flu, snot-caked pants, and ringworm. Oh yes...I said ringworm. But alas, pee, runny noses, and wadded up tissues are my life. I know, you're probably at home shaking your head at me and thinking, "You silly girl. When are you going to realize that you have chosen to work in an incubator of germs and snot?"

WHILE I HAVE resigned myself to dealing with *some* aforementioned bodily fluids, there are still some that I prefer to keep out of the classroom. Like poop. And puke, barf, boot…whatever you like to call it. For some reason, the kids at my school puke *all the time*. I do not remember so much puke in my own elementary school years. I chalk it up to the declining quality of cafeteria food combined with a steady diet of Reese's Peanut Butter Cups for breakfast.

Usually there is a warning when someone is about to blow chunks. They will raise their hand with their other hand clutched across their mouth. Or start to dry heave. Or just run out of the classroom, leaving me to assume it had to be pretty urgent.

Shortly after my poo-soaked friend cleared out of the room, a little girl calmly raised her hand (which shows she was listening when we talked about how screaming doesn't get things done any faster…love you, sweetheart) and said, "Mrs. Mimi, I need to throw up."

To which I replied, "Do you think you can make it?" and then added my own silent prayer for patience. I mean, come on! Both ends in one day?!

She nods her head yes, and with my blessing is soon off to boot all over the bathroom. When she returns, she looks pretty foul. I decide that she doesn't look ready to puke and rally (a term I'm sure many of you are familiar with from the college years...) and so I send her to the nurse with a friend. I scribble out a note on a nearby Post-it and send the girls on their way.

Several minutes later the girls return and Pukey Patty looks a bit worse for wear.

"Mrs. Mimi, we went to the nurse's office but she said we needed to come back to class to get an Official Pass."

"What?! She actually sent you back for an Official Pass?!" I said in an incredulous tone, my voice dripping with moderate sarcasm here.

"Yes. She said you should know better than to send her a note on regular paper."

"Let me get this straight. You handed her my note about Pukey Patty and she sent you back to class?"

"Yes."

"Is Pukey Patty okay? She doesn't look so good..."

"She threw up again. But the nurse told us to leave, so I took her to the bathroom to do it."

"Ah, I see. That was some smart thinking, honey. Way to problem solve!" I send the two girls back down to the nurse's office after digging up an Official Pass.

Ten minutes later, the girls returned once again.

"What's the problem now?"

"The nurse says Patty isn't really sick enough. She wrote you a note."

"Let me see it." I open the note and read, "I do not have the facilities to handle children that are not really sick. Please handle your students yourself."

Oh no she didn't.

Is this my punishment for pawning off my shit-stained little friend on Ms. Know It All?

Approximately 30 seconds after I finish reading the nurse's ridiculous note, Pukey Patty barfs again. A lot. But this time, my poor little friend managed to make it to the trash can. She's such a good girl.

Then, despite my better judgment, I send Pukey Patty and her friend back down to the nurse for a third time. This time they carried the trash can full of boot with them. They also carried an Official Pass which read, "Is she sick enough now?"

And wouldn't you know it…but my little helper came back to class alone and poor Pukey Patty mercifully got to go home. Only two more hours until I get to go home and lay down, too. Sigh. It has been a long week.

I LIKE TO BE ahead of the game. I plan at least two weeks in advance. When we go on vacation, I am already planned for the week we get back. I don't like pulling lessons out of my behind at the last minute. I feel most successful when I can look at my planner for the coming week and it is filled with notes, colorful Post-its, and lists. To me, that signals that I have put in some serious thought and am thoroughly prepared to get as much out of the week as I possibly can despite all the interruptions. After all, I am expected to essentially squeeze ten hours of learning into six actual classroom hours. There have been desperate times when I have rationalized that lunch is not necessary, for me or the kids, because we have so much stuff to get through. Relax, I've never actually withheld food from children, but that doesn't mean I haven't thought about it.

Our days are intense. I am on them from the second they walk in the door to the second they walk back out of it. This is partially because an intense amount of pressure is put on *me* to cover an insane amount of material, and shit rolls downhill.

Our reading specialists say, "All teachers should spend a two to three hour block of time on literacy."

Our math specialists say, "The city mandates sixty to ninety minutes of math daily."

The Visionary says I should be engaging in science instruction for at least 45 minutes a day.

And don't forget about social studies: We must get an hour of social studies a day.

Oh, and small group instruction in areas of deficit.

Ooooh, and don't forget to bring them to the library!

Yikes. We really should get in some art instruction… don't forget about that!

Oh, right, and have you been keeping up with your assessing?

Okay, *everybody hold it*! Has anyone with any common sense ever added up all of these demands and realized that they equal more hours than actually exist in a typical school day? Huh, geniuses? Ever think outside of your own specialized box? I'm guessing no. And yes, I realize that each of those demands are totally valid. And that each individual interruption is really no big deal in the grand scheme of things. Hey, if the kids miss Readers' Workshop once because of a last-minute assembly, that's cool. But it's when you *add up* all those interruptions, those last-minute change of plans, and incessant demands on our time that I feel like I'm going to explode!

Our administration tells us to just "be flexible." At this point, eight years into my "flexibility," I feel a bit like a human pretzel. Why do our classroom schedules always seem like the last priority? Here's a finger snapper: Maybe, just maybe, what the *teacher* does in her classroom should be at the center of the school and everything else should happen around that. So instead of us trying to do our jobs in spite of all the disruptions, people outside the classroom might spend their times thinking of ways that our instruction can be augmented by other experiences or at least carefully consider how important our daily interactions with children truly are before they pick up the phone.

NVIGORATED BY MY 154th Positive Attitude Pep Talk with myself, I promptly created a new classroom job on our Helping Hands chart: The Operator. The Operator is in charge of answering the classroom phone and taking messages. They are to answer the phone with a cheerful "We're learning!" It is a thing of beauty.

Ring!

OPERATOR: "We're learning!"

ANGRY VOICE: "Uh, what?"

OPERATOR: "We're learning!"

ANGRY VOICE: (clearly thrown off) "Oh, well, okay. It can wait."

I thought so. Touché, angry voice, touché.

THE FUNNY THING about teaching is that even after a week filled with disruption after disruption, the next week always shines like a glimmer of hope in the distance. Hope that maybe my friends and I will be able to have a day or two of uninterrupted learning together. I think it is that hope that keeps me going most of the time...

Unfortunately, my bubble of hope for next week is burst by the realization that it is time for us to start rehearsing for the second grade assembly. (Imagine me turning the page of my planner, seeing a Post-it note that reads *start rehearsals*, and then slowly lowering my head down onto the table. Am I crying? A little.) It is safe to say that the biggest disruption to learning of all is the dog and pony show that is more commonly referred to as an all-school assembly. I know that the assembly is part of the trappings that make up elementary school: you know, with other things like glue sticks, sporks, and spelling tests. But every year at this time, I find myself questioning our school's priorities and wondering if they include student learning. There are just too many moments where I feel as if we are parading around Everything We Can Do, while really, we aren't doing anything very well. Combine the reality of our impending assembly with the approaching winter break, and you have a recipe for disaster!

Let me take this opportunity to say I HATE ASSSEMBLIES!

I need to calm down. I mean, what's the big deal? They're nothing to get worked up about. We just have to come up with a theme, find some songs, plan a few transitions, teach the kids their parts, make some costumes, write and print up programs, coordinate rehearsals, and get 80 seven-year-old children to do it all independently while we teachers squat behind chairs in the first row. Piece of cake! I apologize for overreacting.

What I am trying to say (if you didn't pick up on that heavy sarcasm there) is that assemblies are the biggest pain-in-the-neck circus act ever! We might as well just ask the children to jump through hula hoops lit on fire and call it a day. And just before you thought it couldn't get any worse, friends, enter our music teacher, Mr. Big White Guitar. I'm not entirely sure what he does during the day, either. I am fairly certain that he is not actively teaching music because my class has been working on the same song for at least three years now. Honestly, I have this theory that there is a secret coffee lounge area where the music teacher, The Weave, and The Fanny Pack all hang out between 8 and 3. And, as God as my witness, I will find where that coffee bar is and what is in that fanny pack if it kills me.

Mr. Big White Guitar earned his name by always carrying a big, white guitar. But it's not so much that he always carries said guitar, because he's a music teacher, so it's not really that ridiculous. What gets me is that he uses his big, white guitar to accompany our little cherubs at every single assembly. And despite the fact that he is *completely* unoccupied from the hours of 9 to 11, his big white guitar remains untuned in time for our perform-ance every single time. I guess if I had all morning to hang out in the mystery coffee bar/slacker hole I would be hard-pressed to find the time to turn those little knobby things and strum my strings. Seriously, I have got to stop having such high expectations for others.

As a result of Mr. Big White Guitar's failure to do his job the following takes place year after year.

Setting: A sweaty un-air-conditioned sauna/auditorium. Two hundred restless children aged three to nine sit anxiously anticipating the impending display of theatrical genius. Sprinkled throughout the crowd are several teachers, frantically signaling things to their class. Between all the thumbs-ups, hand waving, shushing, and pointing you'd think they were trying to wave in an airplane to land, but no, what they're really doing is trying to get their 20 children to wait patiently in their seats and *not* ask to go to the bathroom. All four second-grade teachers, including myself, are squatting in the front row waving kids on and shooting alternating looks of encouragement and looks of death at our little friends: It's truly a display of pedagogical brilliance.

ME: (in that weird teacher whisper/hiss) "Go! Go! Go! You can do it! You look awesome! Don't forget to smile! Stand up straight! Look smart! Get ready to sing! Eyes on me! Don't touch your partner!"

Now that I think about it, I'm firing directions at them like an idiot possessed, like they're even listening.

Please. They are way too busy looking for their parents, and picking their noses.

MY SUPER COLLEAGUE: "Okay guys! Get ready! Eyes on me! Smile! Smile! Nice and loud now!"

A few more evil glances, some desperate hand waving, and we're set! Yes! Yes! They're perfect! They look so cute! It was totally all worth it! All the extra hours, the rehearsals, the anxiety-induced stomachaches. They're beautiful. I think I feel a tear welling up in my eye when...

There's silence. Absolute silence. We have successfully gotten 80 small children to file onto stage into four perfect rows on risers. The crowd is anxiously awaiting their harmonic little voices raised in song, yet all we hear is...THAT JERK TUNING HIS GUITAR!

At this point the 80 children who just moments ago had me close to tears of joy are now in their full glory, pushing one another, talking, waving at the audience, and definitely not smiling and looking at the teacher. Eventually, the guitar gets tuned (way to go, jerk!), the children start singing, and the whole thing is over, but I can't help but wonder sometimes...why do I even bother?

I need to go upstairs, sit down, and turn the page of my planner...winter break is just a few precious days away.

So, IMAGINE FOR a moment the day before the holiday break. For those of you who don't teach, it's like keeping a lid on a boiling pot of insanely over-excited crazy people. My friends are sugared up, sleep deprived, overexcited, and counting the minutes until the end of the day. We have completed the requisite holiday-non-religious-or-overly-specific craft and are shining with a fresh coat of glue and glitter. Bags are packed, holiday homework packets are passed out, and there are STILL 15 minutes before I can bring them downstairs to be dismissed (damn!). Being FIVE minutes early makes you look on top of your shit, but being 15 minutes early to the auditorium makes you look like a strung out, lazy jerk and you know I'm all about appearances.

And in that 15 minutes, I made the fatal mistake of agreeing to open my presents in front of the class.

Keep in mind, I have taught for seven years. I should know better.

Shame on me.

We gather on the carpet. Quite a few children have generously brought me a gift this year. Honestly, I don't expect much and would be very happy with a thoughtful drawing or something, but many of my parents are amazing and have sent something in. I even have one friend who saved his allowance for three weeks to buy a gift for me. I mean, COME ON!

We are mid love-fest as I unwrap the usual mugs, scented candles, and assorted lotions and soaps. Apparently I smell. But I am choosing not to be offended. Everyone is excited and giggly as I unwrap their gift. Then I get to a beautifully wrapped shirt box from my friend who we will call Braids. (She always has them.) Braids can barely contain herself.

BRAIDS: "Open it! Just rip off the paper!"

ME: "But it's so pretty…"

BRAIDS: "I picked it out myself. For you…"

ME: "That's very sweet."

BRAIDS: "It's for Mr. Mimi too." (That was a KEY piece of information. Also remember that she said she picked this out HERSELF.)

I pull out the box and open the lid as Braids practically pees in her pants because she is so excited…

It's… (Oh my God!)

(Are you sitting down?)

A BRIGHT RED NIGHTIE AND A BLACK G-STRING! I am so serious.

It's okay. Take a moment. I had to.

ME: "Wow! How lovely!" (Which I managed to say as I scramble to put the lingerie back into the box a.s.a.p. so that EVERYONE doesn't have the opportunity to bask in this gift's inappropriate glory.)

BRAIDS: "My mom says you can use it to have babies."

Oh dear. I guess it's the thought that counts?

Finding My Zen...

I ALSO CONSIDERED NAMING this chapter "The Art of Being Zen-ful" for all of you fans of *The Hills* out there, but re-thought this personal homage to Justin Bobby at the last minute. How do I have so much time to stay so au courant with reality television you ask? It's called DVR, people, DVR and a whole heck of a lot of dedication (read: denial of all the work I actually have to do until the last minute). It's just how I roll.

It is the first week back after our Christmas vacation (Whoops! Sorry, I meant Winter Holiday), and Monday through Wednesday have been super. I am rested and uber-prepared! I spent one whole day of my vacation planning and prepping for the following week and am feeling pretty good about myself. The kids are pumped to be back, too, and we are just rocking out together. My read alouds are rockin', the projects are fun, the kids are engaged...it is like learning is pouring out of us. This is when I love my job.

But by Thursday, by Thursday I feel like I should just run off and join the circus because (a) it is a way out of all the ridiculousness, and (b) my administration's pleas to "be flexible" at all times have practically rendered me a freaking contortionist, so I might have a new career on the horizon. How is it that *my* schedule is always everyone's last concern? Things that I plan to do with my friends *always* come second to the demands of everyone who floats around outside of the classroom. Everyone asks me to understand, "just this once," but all those once's add up to a change in our schedule at least three times a week. And just like that, our week goes from being packed with learning to totally f*cked up (pardon my language, but there's no other way to describe it...so much for Being Positive in 2009). Before I know it, it will be June and I will be three months behind. And then the administration will look at *me*, and ask me why I didn't get through my curriculum.

If they would just spend a minute looking at my friends and me when we are really jamming, maybe the administration would realize that *this* is what is most important. That what we do together in our classrooms is what schools are all about. Concerts, visitors, professional development, committee meetings, and assemblies are all just icing on the cake. Unfortunately, we seem to always have way too much icing and not enough cake.

Rather than cater to the needs of all the adults who don't work directly with children, I want to focus on catering to the needs of my friends. I mean, correct me if I'm wrong, but that's what I get paid to do, right? I get paid to focus on *them*, plan for *them*, be prepared for *them*. Right now, however, it feels like I get paid to be a human shield to protect my friends from all the chaos and drama that happens outside the walls of our classroom. I absorb all the bullshit, swallow it down, and put on a happy face for my friends as I desperately try to keep us moving forward despite all the last-minute changes to our day.

I spent the weekend with one of my girlfriends who is very new agey. She talked a lot about being Zen, and finding her Zen. Sometimes I think this Zen business is a bunch of crap, but I felt like it couldn't hurt to try to find mine at this point.

So, this last week I focused on finding my Zen, assuming that it had been lost somewhere, like a misplaced pencil or something, and if I just tried hard enough, I would find it again.

I thought my mission was a lost cause when I was told

we had a surprise concert that really had been planned months in advance but no one had bothered to tell the teachers, so I guess the surprise part was just for us. Surprise! Scrap your plans! Be flexible!

If I become any more flexible, I swear I may run off and join Cirque du Soleil. I bet they're Zen. I know I keep saying it, but one of these days, watch out!

So we're at the *surprise!* concert, which is a Brazilian drumming group. And not only am I lamenting this "oversight in communication" (that's what the office calls it; they say "oversight in communication"; I say yet another screwup from a bunch of morons), I am also lamenting having had four glasses of wine the previous evening with my Zen friend. Now, I never have more than a glass during the week, because I am not a huge drinker (read: I am old and can't handle it anymore). But I made an exception because a very old friend was in town and catching up is just so much better over several glasses of good Cabernet. Long story short, the change in schedule hurt, the drumming hurt even more, and I was definitely not feeling Zen.

And then the lady on stage started dancing. She had fabulously untamed curly hair and wasn't wearing any shoes, which is usually a big old check in the minus column if you ask me, but somehow seemed fitting for her. She danced to the music shaking her shaky thing, and was totally into it. I'm sure her shaky thing had some sort of name that we were supposed to learn during the course of the concert but there was just so much banging that I had trouble focusing...or caring. At first I thought she was ridiculous and lame. I mean honestly, most people who perform in elementary schools are one small step from multicolored turtlenecks, suspenders, and that weird sing-songy this-is-how-I-think-you-are-supposed-to-talk-to-kids voice. But then I realized that she was just super into it. And super-talented. And probably could not have cared less what I thought of her anyway, because she clearly loved what she was doing.

Suddenly, I want to be the dancing lady with the shaky thing. She had found her Zen.

Later we were in the classroom, totally rocking out our math centers. Kids were (finally) making smart choices and starting to internalize all my talk (read: rambling) about taking responsibility for their own learning. At one point, when my small little cologne-spritzed current favorite, Mr. Suave, chose the money game, articulating that he chose it because he knows counting money is hard for him and he wants to improve, I almost had to wipe away a tear. (I can be that schmaltzy, and I'm proud of it!)

And I realized, I am in my Zen place. With a shaky thing. Okay, not literally a shaky thing, but doing what I want to do. I just get so bogged down by all the crap. Let me define crap: "oversight in communication," jacked-up copy orders, bat-shit crazy parents, the administrative obsession with hard numbers over actual people... that I forget about the kids. Which is so sad, because although I hate it when people tell me to "do it for the kids," I do love my kids. And when they act bat-shit crazy, forget to tell me something, or screw up an assignment, at least it's because they're *children* and still learning.

I think I have found my Zen. It is with the kids.

So, like a true adult professional, I decide to ignore everyone I work with outside of my classroom. I shut the door and leave all the complaining, gossiping, laziness, and drama in the hall. Yeah, I'm engaging in the Silent Treatment, Adult Style. And it's very Zen.

I AM DEEP INTO ignoring everyone with whom I work. Everyone except my kids and my Super Colleagues, that is. And it's kind of working. I'm feeling very Zen. And Lord knows this place tries to destroy one's Zen at every possible twist and turn. We are back to having fun together and I am able to loosen up a bit and really enjoy spending the day with them. I may actually be (gasp!) fun to be around. Actually I have been spending so much time ignoring adults and hanging out with kids that I may have forgotten that they are actually *not* mini-adults. Perhaps even worse, I have been having so much fun that I may have also forgotten that I am the adult in this scenario. Yeah, I'm still planning and doing all my adult responsibilities, but I am so deeply nerdy that all of this feels fun, too.

This afternoon, I was cruelly reminded that I am the adult. I think that all of us who work in the public school system are familiar with the phenomenon of post-lunch gas. I am particularly familiar with the gas that erupts from those friends who eat the free and reduced "lunch." In my situation, that would be 90 percent of my whole class. Some days, it can be downright toxic on the carpet.

(Just to clarify here, I'm not talking about the elusive but ever-present Teacher Fart because that could be a whole chapter in and of itself. And you teachers out there, don't act like you don't know what I'm talking about, either. You know you've dropped a bomb on a kid and then quickly found a reason to walk away to attend to something else clear on the other side of the room, leaving the poor child to gasp for air and promptly blame the children around him.)

Today must have been an unusually potent day in the cafeteria because we had an "incident" after lunch. To get you up to speed, we recently planted grass seed in three different soil samples to determine the type of soil that is best for plant growth. Pretty gnarly, I know, but my kids are rock stars if I do say so myself. And I do...often. On Friday, the grass was about half an inch high. Today it was three inches tall and darn impressive. Again, they are rock stars.

Most of the kids noticed the grass as soon as they walked in the room. (Seriously, have you ever noticed the radar on some kids? You move a certain poster half an inch to the left and they notice *and* comment on it...profusely...to the point where sometimes adding new stuff to the classroom is just annoying because you know it will result in some high drama the next morning.) Remember, I said *most* kids are quick to notice these changes, not all. There are always a few who remain comfortably unaware of what is going on around them.

I have one such friend in my class. He is a pudgy little guy with big eyes and the longest eyelashes you've ever seen. Really, he's very cute except he is insanely *slow* to follow simple directions. He's very, very smart but just very slow and methodical in every single excruciating movement he makes. Honestly, he's lucky he has those eyelashes...

Anyway, we had just gotten back from lunch when I addressed the grass samples.

Most of the kids had noticed the change in the grass earlier that morning and so were not shocked when they saw it, just anxious to talk about it. Evidently, Luscious Lashes had not noticed the grass that morning and when I took the samples down from the bookshelf, I rocked Luscious Lashes' world.

He got so excited about the grass that he exclaimed, "Wow!" Evidently all the excitement and force he used to exclaim "wow" coincided with a raging gas attack because he practically blew two of my girls off the rug!

It was like his fart ripped time and space in half. Afterward, a stunned silence filled the room. Children's eyes darted madly around the room, hands covered mouths in desperate attempts to not laugh. After all, we have had the Everybody Farts talk multiple times already this year. Well, everybody farts but the teacher, that is.

Unfortunately, I couldn't hold it together. Me. The grown-up.

I laughed. They laughed. Luscious Lashes even laughed. And that was it. I'm glad Lashes has a good sense of humor.

The next day, during those 15 minutes when we choke down our food before dashing back to our classrooms, a period of time known to many of you as *lunch*, I regaled my Super Colleagues with the tale of The Fart That

Rocked the Rug. I had everyone in stitches. I mean, who doesn't love a good fart story? Yes, teachers tell fart stories at lunch. Get over it.

Wait a minute. Maybe I can let my Super Colleagues into me Circle of Zen. After all, working with them and having their support has been a literal lifeline to me over the last few years. I share my thoughts with them and we make a pact. No more talking about anything negative at "lunch." From now on, we will reserve one day a week for complaints and spend the rest of our time enjoying our little friends and one another. Perhaps then we can outwit all the challenges put between us and our Zen every day.

For my first Zen challenge, I was subjected to extremely hot temperatures. Today it was officially 89 degrees in my classroom. Yes, 89. I'm thinking about dressing everyone up in grass skirts and just having a luau. You know, for ha-has. I am definitely sweating my Zen off. If one can even do that...

I was snuggled up to a little friend today, chatting about her writing, when I felt beads of sweat rolling down my back. And I thought to myself, "Self, it's February and you're sweating through your *sleeveless shirt!*" I then glanced at the radiator, which was pumping out heat at such an intense level that you could actually see it rising up in front of the windows. Four of which were open.

Again, it is February and today it was only 38 degrees outside.

For some reason I will never understand, The Visionary commanded our custodial staff to crank up the heat prior to our parent teacher conferences about two weeks ago. Maybe he wanted to sweat them out, maybe he wanted to show off the radiators, maybe he's trying to lose a few pounds...who knows. All I know is it is freaking hot.

Creeping around my bedroom and picking an outfit at 5:30 in the morning in the dark so Mr. Mimi can sleep is hard enough without throwing in the extra challenge of choosing something that has enough layers to keep me warm on the commute as well as cool in the classroom. Plus, I have shelf after shelf of fabulous, wooly sweaters (I have a winter birthday...and am on the spoiled side, so seriously, I'm talking about a hideous number of sweaters here) that I have been fantasizing about ever since I decided I was sick of my summer wardrobe.

So now, not only am I mourning my inability to wear my favorite winter wear, but I am also dealing with chronic bloody noses (if you are a student teacher or new to teaching, you need to be real with yourself about the sheer amount and varied types of bodily fluids you are about to encounter; you'll thank me later because no one else will warn you about this stuff), sleepy children, and abandoned sweaters piled up in all corners of the classroom. In the last week alone I have said the phrase, "Put your clothes back on" more times than I care to admit as children attempt to strip down to their undershirts.

And every time I picture the germs that must be breeding in our sweltering sweatbox of a classroom, I think I might hurl.

Yesterday I finally thought to ask The Visionary if we could turn down the heat. You know, just a smidge. My request was met with a resounding, "It's either on or off!" which I find very hard to believe since I witnessed a custodian turn it up myself. I mean, if there's an up, there's a down, friend. As I left the office, I heard the secretary mutter under her breath, "Those teachers, always complaining."

Nice.

Maybe I'll just turn this negative into a positive and embrace the sweating. You know, I'll sweat off a few holiday pounds and be ready for bikini season by the time June arrives. See? I can be an optimist, too. I can feel my Zen returning already.

THANK GOODNESS FOR the restorative powers of my students. We had all sufficiently stripped down to our T-shirts and were in the midst of Writer's Workshop. I was moving around the room, conferencing with various friends and checking the progress of their work. One little girl, who I will call Little Diva, was working on a cover for her latest story.

"Hey, Little Diva, how's it going?" I ask. "Did you come up with a good title for your story?"

She pushes her cover toward me, too immersed in her illustrations to look up.

I pick up her cover. Carefully drawn bubble letters form the words My F*cker. Complete with a backward "c."

My *F*cker? What?!*

"Um, sweetheart, can *you* read me the title you chose?" I ask innocently, praying that she won't say what I think she might say. I mean, she's saucy, but that's a little too saucy, even for her.

"It's called 'My Future.'"

"Oh, 'My *Future*'! What a great title!" I say, the relief evident in my voice.

"Yeah, it's about how I want to be a singer when I grow up. I was in a concert at church last month."

"Wow! 'Future' is a big word. Tell me, did you sound that out on your own?"

"Yeah! I heard 'f' for the first sound, then a short 'u' sound, but I got stuck in the middle. I think 'c-k' makes the 'ch' sound and then 'e-r' says 'er' at the end." She looks up at me beaming, clearly proud of her ability to sound out a word.

"Hey, super star! That's great! But you know what? Sometimes when writer's get to a really hard word in their title, they ask their teachers for help, because titles are really important. Here's how you spell 'future.'" I pass her a Post-it note with the word.

"But you never spell words for us..." Little Diva says, clearly confused.

"I know, honey, but just this once I'm going to. Here's a new paper for your cover." I hand her some new paper and quickly remove her old cover before anyone can try to read it and perhaps sound it out more successfully.

Where is the Zen in all this you ask? Well, I found great joy in color copying this little gem and sending it out to my teacher friends everywhere.

*n*OT SURPRISINGLY, MY Zen was challenged yet again the following week, and once again, it was my friends to the rescue. You see, I have a bit of a mouse problem in my classroom. I don't have any food in the room, but somehow, they seem to migrate to me. I don't blame my school for this one. After all, it's New York City and mice are everywhere. I just prefer not to have them so in my face.

Because we're a public school, we're not allowed to use poison to kill the mice. Something about children and poison...Anyhow, we have to use sticky traps instead. After a recent episode in which I found a mouse crawling around under my bulletin board paper (true story, evidently they can walk up walls), I asked the custodian to put some sticky traps around my room. I came in early the next morning to get some paperwork done and was greeted by a truly gruesome sight.

In the night, a mouse had gotten two of its paws stuck in the sticky trap. It had used its other two paws to drag itself out of the corner of the room and right to the middle of my carpet. Evidently exhausted from the effort, the mouse gave up and, although it was still somewhat alive, two other little mice had come to begin to eat him.

And good morning to me!

Screaming, I ran down the hall for some help. Or a Xanax. Whatever came first. People who have found their Zen do not need Xanax.

But in true rock star–teacher fashion, I swallowed my horror (and *not* a Xanax, just in case you were wondering) and picked up my class after the carcass had been cleared away. Once the kids were unpacked (they remained completely unaware of the ghastly acts that had transpired just a few moments prior to their entry), I asked Bubbles to work on a special project at the back of the classroom with another little girl we will call Smarty Pants. They are independent and basically total superstars so I knew I could trust them.

The rest of my friends were on the carpet when Smarty Pants enthusiastically raised her hand and said, "We need help!"

Thinking that they just needed more paint or something, I said, "What is it?"

Smarty Pants answered, "Bubbles just peed all over herself and the floor and we need help with the puddle."

That is so not what I thought she was going to say. Of *course* that's the problem. Urine is just what I need to make my tenuous hold on my Zen disappear completely.

Oddly though, no one laughed or said anything. I knew they heard Smarty Pants. So what was the deal? Was this empathy? A mature response? Or perhaps, is no one even listening?

I quickly send the rest of the group back to their seats and make my way to the back of the classroom to check out Bubbles and her now infamous puddle. Expecting to find her sobbing behind the art center, I am surprised when I see her diligently painting away, with her pants rolled up to her knees to stay out of the puddle, acting as if nothing has happened.

ME: "Bubbles, are you okay? What happened?"

BUBBLES: (enthusiastically) "I *burst!*"

ME: (trying not to laugh) "Why didn't you ask to go to the bathroom?"

BUBBLES: "I was so into the project that I just didn't."

ME: (shocked that Bubbles is handling this better than I am) "What can I do to help you?"

BUBBLES: "You know anyone who can take care of this?" (Indicates puddle of pee.)

ME: "Um, yeah (still trying not to laugh). But what can I do for *you*? Do you want to go to the bathroom and I'll call mom?"

BUBBLES: "Sounds good...let me just finish this up."

And she happily goes back to painting. A couple of minutes later, she cleans off her paintbrush, nimbly leaps over her own pee, and heads to the bathroom.

When Mom arrives with a clean pair of pants, I tell her the story. Mom and I have a good laugh while Bubbles goes to the bathroom yet again, this time to change. It is close to the end of the day, so I tell her it is okay if she wants to go home with Mom. She insists on staying in school, stating, "Hey, it was just a little pee."

Genius, I think. Bubbles is very Zen. These words of wisdom from my little friend are what carry me through the next few weeks. When I am freaking out about my mouse-filled classroom or the antics of The Bacon Hunter, I will think, "Hey, it's all just a little pee."

I T'S MY BIRTHDAY today. Last year I turned thirty and ROCOed in Vegas with my best girlies. I had my suitcase packed in the back of my classroom, stared longingly at it all day, and took off as soon as the kids left. This year I am turning 31 and it no longer seems so hot. I don't mind being in my thirties (it's actually kinda nice), but 31 is a bit anti-climatic after all the 30 hoopla.

Now don't get me wrong. I *love* birthdays...or at least,

I love *my* birthday. Like most women, I believe it should actually be a month-long celebration of me rather than one short day. I like to stretch out the singing, clapping, and gift giving as much as possible. But this year, I just couldn't get it up for my birthday.

As I got dressed to come to work this morning, I picked out a fabulous new shirtdress, a super shiny patent belt, and some of my fave high heels. I thought I might as well look the part. Mr. Mimi got up and made me breakfast, wishing me a happy birthday as I ran out the door to catch my train. Yet somehow, especially as I sat sandwiched between two commuters, it did not seem like a special day.

The moment I stepped on the block leading up to school, I was almost bowled over by one of my normally very quiet friends. We both slipped on the treacherous patches of ice that dot the sidewalks like an obstacle course and almost totally bit it.

"Happy Birthday, Mrs. Mimi!" she cried, hugging my legs.

Yeah, I put my birthday on the classroom calendar. In all honesty, my birthday was the first one to be posted on our January calendar. I carefully placed the special birthday magnet on my calendar square and then shamelessly asked the class, "Oh, do any of you have January birthdays, too?" I may be 31, but I still want a special magnet on my special day. Hey, I spend all day celebrating every time a kid even looks studious, I might as well celebrate myself one day out of 180.

After my near-fatal hug, the day went on as normal. I shook each of my friend's hands at the door and said "Good morning," stopping to chat with a few like I always do. But today, there was this weird energy in the group and I thought to myself, "Shit, they're going to be squirrelly today." As I walked in the classroom, I heard a furiously whispered "1, 2, 3…"

And then all 20 of my friends burst into the most beautiful version of "Happy Birthday" you have ever heard. All of a sudden there were cards pulled out of backpacks and even some cookies sent in by someone's family. Because I am a huge sap, I definitely cried a little.

"Thanks you, guys. I've never had a class do that for me before."

The Apple Doesn't Fall Far from the Educational Example

THIS WEEK IS Parent-Teacher Conferences week. This week brings with it many small joys, such as The Joy of Plastering a Smile on My Face for Three Hours as I Tell You That Your Child Is Consistently Showing Little to No Effort, or The Joy of Watching You Refuse to Discipline Your Child in Productive Ways, and finally, The Joy of Acting Like It Doesn't Piss Me Off When You Answer Your Cell Phone in the Middle of Our Conference While Other Parents Wait in the Hall.

So much joy...I almost don't know how to contain myself. Yet somehow I manage.

Now I'm not being fair here. It is also filled with lovely conversations with amazing parents who blow me away with how hard they work to make a good life for their children. These conferences are fabulous: lots of laughing and exchanging of stories. I look forward to spending some time with these parents. But of course these conferences are easy. These are the students who are getting wonderful support at home and therefore are doing beautifully in school. Their parents write back when I send a note home. They fill out field trip permission slips thoroughly and return them before they're due. They show up to their conference on time, and call if they can't make it. These parents truly are a joy.

Sadly, these parents will not get as much attention in the following pages because, really, being lovely and thoughtful just isn't as funny. Also, I'm often too focused on the parents who drive me nuts.

Parent Teacher Conferences is a very special time of the year. It is the time of year where schools put on some of the most impressive dog and pony shows you can imagine. Seriously, the sheer pageantry is amazing. Imagine teachers dressed in their finest "teacher clothes," all their errant piles are shoved into a closet, desks are so clean you could eat off them (or at least the mice do), and the hallways are adorned with fresh new "oh-shit-I-have-to-get-this-up-FAST" bulletin boards. Sometimes I think we should just go all the way, put on some feathered headdresses and do a kick line in the auditorium just to spice things up a bit.

There are many analogies out there that claim to capture what it is like to be a teacher in today's classroom. There is the ever popular analogy that likens the school to a business in which students and families are the clients and teachers become service providers or something equally sterile. Then there is the battle zone analogy that turns the classroom into the "front line" and, I suppose, makes me a warrior. And while I like the idea of being perceived as pretty badass and most likely clad in a fabulously figure-friendly camo pantsuit, I don't think that this analogy accurately represents the Parent Teacher Conference experience, either. Let me go out on a limb and make an analogy for those of you out there who aren't teachers and haven't experienced the joys of Parent Teacher Conference night from the teacher's perspective. Parent Teacher Conference night is like a three-ring circus. As I have said before, I am the trained seal desperately trying to balance a ball on her nose (a.k.a. maintain my professional smile) while simultaneously clapping my fins and barking my heart out (a.k.a. getting parents to take me seriously any way humanly possible). Our Master of Ceremonies is The Visionary, who interrupts our flow with several deafening announcements throughout the night. I think that all principals secretly relish these evenings as a chance to show off their schools, their teachers, and their monopoly over the intercom. Side note: if and when I do decide to quit, I am *totally* grabbing that microphone and making an announcement. That, and I'm going to pull the fire alarm...just once.

In the name of beating an analogy to death, there are also interesting sideshow acts that parents can visit before or after they see their child's teacher. Our school corrals these acts into the gym for easy access and maximum impact. For example, they can go see The World's Biggest Waste of Space (you might remember her as The Fanny Pack), hop over to The Laziest Woman Alive (The Bacon Hunter), or check out some of The World's Most Flexible Women (more commonly known as my other Super Colleagues).

Then there are the acts that are reserved for the three rings: in our school we save that kind of spotlight for the parents. After all, it is their night to shine.

In the first ring we have the Excuse Maker...you know, that parent who when forced to talk about something their child has done will, without fail, give an excuse as to why it was not their precious baby's fault.

ME: "Your child hasn't passed in a completed homework assignment yet this year."

EXCUSE MAKER: "Oh, well it was *my* fault that Little Angel didn't do their homework. Not his."

ME: "But she's in second grade and should be able to do it independently. The assignments for each week are fairly similar on purpose. We have gone over them several times in class. And it's March."

EXCUSE MAKER: "Well, you forgot to remind her to do her homework before she left that day."

ME: (They have homework every night, you want me to remind her to do it every night? Let me choose another battle...) "Okay, well I'd like to talk about your child's behavior lately. I am concerned because recently she has been stealing things out of other children's..."

EXCUSE MAKER: "My little Little Angel would never take something from another child's desk! How dare you?"

ME: "But I saw her do it with my own eyes and then she lied about it...I'm concerned that..."

EXCUSE MAKER: "No! No! She did not take it. Whatever it was! I do not care what you saw! I know someone must have *told* her to do it."

ME: "I just think we should talk about this so that..."

EXCUSE MAKER: "Did you ever think about what *you* did to provoke her to steal from other children?"

(sigh)

In the center ring, we have the Amazing Rubber Parent. I know what you're thinking. You're thinking, "Rubber parent? Man, she has taken this circus analogy *way* too far! Tone it down, woman!" But stick with me for a moment here. The Amazing Rubber Parents are the parents who allow all comments about their child's educational progress to bounce right off of them and smack me right in the face. Particularly if that something I have to say is not all rainbows and kittens. These are the parents who believe it is solely my responsibility to educate their child. And while, yes, I should shoulder a hefty amount of this job, I also believe that some portion should belong to the parents themselves. Call me crazy.

You still with me?

I have one friend who does *not* like math…or working hard for that matter. She's the type of child who will do *anything* to look busy when in reality, she is doing absolutely nothing productive. You know the type of friend to which I refer.

So one day last week we're working with coins and the children have to come up with two ways to show a given amount using quarters, dimes, nickels, and pennies. This is something that they have all done before, today is simply a refresher so that we can move on to more difficult concepts.

You can then imagine my surprise when my friend had done absolutely *nothing* in 20 minutes.

ME: "Friend, what's going on? You haven't even started your work."

FRIEND: "I don't know."

ME: "You don't know what? Do you understand what you have to do?"

FRIEND: "I have to show forty-two cents two different ways."

ME: "Yes, so what's up?"

FRIEND: "I used forty-two pennies."

ME: "Great! But let's think of another way, because I know that people don't usually have all those pennies in their pockets. What other coins could you use?"

FRIEND: "I don't know."

ME: "You don't know?"

FRIEND: "I'm confused."

ME: "Okay…well what other coins have we talked about?"

FRIEND: "I don't know any other coins."

ME: "You don't know any other coins?" (We have been talking about coins for the last two weeks! Okay,

okay, calm down, in through the nose, out through the mouth…)

FRIEND: "No."

ME: "Nickels?"

FRIEND: "No."

ME: "But you talked about nickels all last year. And yesterday. And they're on the wall. Come on, I know you can do it!"

FRIEND: "I'm just really confused and this is hard. My father says that the cashier will make change so all I have to do is give them dollars. And my mom says when things are hard, I shouldn't let myself feel frustrated, I should just stop."

So when I talk to the Amazing Rubber Parents about my concerns, I was met with comments such as, "So what are *you* going to do about it?" and "Well, you get paid the big bucks to be the teacher." When I suggest perhaps that the parent supports their child's learning at home with some additional practice counting coins, I am either treated to a series of snorts and guffaws (presumably indicating the outrageousness of this last statement) or to a laundry list of things that parent has to do that do not include actively parenting their child. Ah yes, the sweet sounds of cooperation.

Finally, in the third ring, we have The Multitaskers. Imagine someone riding around on a horse while simultaneously trying to do some acrobatic magic on the horse's back. These are the parents who might answer a cell phone call while I am mid-sentence. Or perhaps they are busy making a grocery list as I go over their child's grades. Hey, I've even had a parent attempt to conduct a conference with me while listening to her iPod — with *both* headphones in.

ME: "So, your child is currently reading slightly below…"

MULTITASKER: (cell phone blowing up in bag) "Where is my phone?" (digging through bag)

ME: "Um, so as I was saying, your child's reading is a bit of a concern. I think that maybe…"

MULTITASKER: (pulling out phone) "Hello? Heeeyyyy! What's up?" (laughing)

ME: "Uh…"

MULTITASKER: (more laughing) "So I'll meet you later? No. Right now I'm at school. With the teacher." (laughing)

ME: (What are they saying?) "Hi, so, there are parents waiting in the hall…"

MULTITASKER: (giving me a half eye roll and pointing at

her phone) "Yeah. (hangs up) So where do I sign? I've got to get going."

Maybe I'm just a jerk who doesn't understand what it is like to be a parent. I just don't think that 15 uninterrupted minutes with your child's teacher is too much to ask for. Or that they know my name. Or what grade I teach.

Now, when I was little, the teacher was almost always right. In fact, I can only remember one occasion in which I got to be right. I was in first grade and my teacher was a total train wreck. She called my mom one day and told her that I had been talking too much in class. Okay, so maybe I was. But so was everyone else. *And...*she neglected to mention that while we were all talking, she was standing outside our classroom *smoking* and watching us through the window! True story.

I, however, am not chain smoking outside my classroom. And I'm not making up stories about children for my own sick personal benefit. I'm telling you about your child so that maybe, just maybe, you can meet me halfway and help your child progress and mature. Just a thought.

THE DAY OF conferences has finally arrived. My To Do list is brimming with all sorts of clean-up tasks, many of which involve shoving stacks of books and papers into empty cabinets. While I am an organizational goddess, I also fall prey to the problem that plagues many teachers: piles of crap everywhere. During my free period, I blow through the remainder of my To Dos with the exception of the last one. My last To Do is simply to vacuum.

When you are an elementary school teacher, vacuuming can be a near orgasmic experience. You see, many of us have colorful rugs on which our little friends gather several times a day to take in our brilliance. Often times these rugs are cheerful corners ripe with memories of gathering as a classroom community. However, there are other times in which these rugs more closely resemble a science experiment gone horribly wrong. Almost like we purposely sprinkled it with various types of bacteria just to see what might happen. Among the debris and funk one might find buttons, torn scraps of paper from a crayon, pee stains, snot wipes, and the always popular "thing from the bottom of someone's shoe." Sprinkle in a little glitter and an old Kleenex and your formerly adorable rug is now a horrifying example of how quickly classrooms accumulate dirt.

For some reason, no matter what state the carpet is in, my friends dutifully sit upon it whenever I ask and never turn up their little noses. In my earlier days as a teacher, I would vacuum the carpet each and every night with my Super Colleagues' vacuum. When that vacuum broke, I bought one for everyone to share. When that vacuum broke, we all chipped in for another hallway vacuum. Are you noticing a pattern here? Teachers pay for and provide vacuums for their classrooms, not the school. Oh, and teachers vacuum the carpets, not the custodial staff. Tired of this cycle of things-that-don't-fall-into-my-job-description, I decided to take a stand and refuse to vacuum my own carpet, thinking that once it got bad enough, someone on the custodial staff would break down and do it, right?

Wrong. Evidently there are some people who vehemently stick to the job description outlined in their contract. Teachers don't have this luxury and are therefore left holding the buck that everyone else has passed.

It has been about two months since I began my Vaccuum Protest. I thought that I would have it in me to hold out, but I don't know. I guess the visions of myself chained to my bookshelves, refusing to vacuum were all in vain. I don't have the balls to let parents come into my classroom and see the monstrosity that currently is my carpet. Because they will blame me. And that might send me over the edge.

However, there isn't a vacuum for as far as the eye can see. I know the custodial staff has one, but they keep it locked in a secure location where it is sure to be as inconvenient as possible. In a bold attempt to keep the Vaccuum Protest 2009 alive, I decide to email The Visionary with my dilemma. After all, he is often the ringleader of our little dog and pony show and I think I can count on him to help me in my quest to keep up appearances.

My email goes as follows:

Just a quick favor. I am wondering if the custodial staff could possibly vacuum the carpets in teachers' classrooms before conferences tonight. I would do it myself, but our floor no longer has a working vacuum. I have already purchased two myself and cannot buy another one, especially before tonight. I know we want to put our best foot forward…thanks in advance!

Mrs. Mimi

And I hit send. That was it. The request was out there. I was officially asking for someone else to work just as hard as my Super Colleagues and I and, just this once, to do something that isn't strictly outlined in their job responsibilities in the name of a community effort. I put it out there. Now all I could do was sit back and watch to see what happens.

Surprise of surprises, our principal says that he will ask the custodial staff to pop around and vacuum our rugs for us, since we have so much going on. And they did…they did vacuum, which I do appreciate. I just wish it wasn't in the middle of my uber-silent Writer's Workshop.

And so, in that moment of quiet, when all 20 of my little friends were diligently writing away, filling me with a sense of pride, and they were hideously interrupted with the incessant noise of a vacuum cleaner, I realized…it's just easier to do it my freaking self.

THE HALLWAYS HAVE been freshly waxed, my desks are spotless, and there are no signs of stray piles of papers anywhere. I am wearing a supercute new dress that says, "I am professional" yet at the same time also makes it clear that, "I am not into thematic sweaters or macaroni necklaces."

I have spent hours preparing notes on each child so that when parents arrive, I am not rendered a smiling fool. My notes are compiled to help me be efficient and thorough in my commentary. In addition, I have a variety of work samples for parents to browse as well as all previously given assessments at the ready. I am alphabetized, sanitized, and energized.

The Visionary makes the announcement for parents to begin heading upstairs. We are poised and ready to speed conference. After all, everyone gets only 15 minutes. I see a familiar face walking down the hall. It is one of my friend's grandfather, an elderly man from Ghana who smiles and waves at me every day. I shuffle through my comments, pull up my friend's report card, and before I know it, his grandfather is seated in front of me. We are ready to go! What a great way to start off the night. This friend is an amazing student. I can be positive and lovely (and really mean it!). Until I realize (insert sound of screeching brakes here) he doesn't speak any English. None. Not a word. So we sit and smile at each other as our 15 precious minutes tick away. My mind is racing. What do I do? I don't want to insult him, but at the same time we're just sitting here grinning like idiots at each other.

I motion toward the report card. He smiles. I point at Peter's grades. He smiles. I give an awkward thumbs-up. He smiles. I apologize for only speaking English. He smiles.

I shrug my shoulders and give him an apologetic look. He gets out his cell phone. He dials. And then he hands me the cell phone. It rings.

OTHER VOICE: "Hello?"

ME: "Hi."

OTHER VOICE: "Who is this?"

ME: "It's Mrs. Mimi."

OTHER VOICE: "Oh, is something wrong? Did something happen?"

ME: "No, no. I'm just here with your father having a conference..."

OTHER VOICE: "Is that tonight? I thought it was tomorrow!"

ME: "It's tomorrow, too. Were you planning on coming tomorrow?"

OTHER VOICE: "Yes. Why is my father there?"

ME: "Um, I think he wants to pick up the report card. Unfortunately, I don't speak..."

OTHER VOICE: "Of course you don't. Can you put him on the phone, please?"

I hand over the phone. He listens for a few minutes, says something, and hangs up. Then he smiles, waves, and leaves the classroom.

So much for all my preparation. I wonder if he noticed the rug?

ONFERENCE NIGHT CHUGS on and surprisingly, I see about 12 parents. My numbers are definitely up from last year. It feels good to sit and talk with the parents, rather than exchange hurried hellos first thing in the morning. It always helps to remind me that my little friends are actually someone else's babies, which makes me care about them even more than I already do. It's especially helpful for my frame of mind when one of those little friends is currently on my shit list. For the most part, the parents who show up are interested in the progress of their child and seem willing to meet me halfway. It's been a good night.

Toward the end of the night, a parent comes rushing in with three small children and one of my friends in tow. We sit down to chat and my friend settles into the library with a favorite book. The other three children, however, begin to run bat-shit crazylike all around my classroom, grabbing at books, markers, and whatever else they can get their hands on. My friend seems nonplussed by this behavior; so does the parent. I, of course, being the behavioral Nazi that I am, am horrified. I look at the parent and smile, an "I'll let you handle this situation" look written clearly all over my face. In return, I receive a blank stare...or is it a challenge? Who will be the first to discipline these children? I am not the parent; however, they are quickly destroying my territory. It is like a western showdown, a behavioral walk off of sorts. You know, all "meet me at the warehouse."

Either way, no one is telling these little darlings that this type of behavior is completely unacceptable in my kingdom. I watch as this mini-friend picks up one of my most favorite picture books and tosses it carelessly on my freshly vacuumed carpet. That's it. I turn around in my chair and shoot the little one my very best Teacher Look. And just like magic, the child stops dead in his tracks, stares back at me for the briefest of moments, and then quickly picks up the book and begins quietly reading.

Ah, I do love a good Teacher Look. I try not to whip it out too often, but sometimes I just can't help myself. Of course, it has just about a 100 percent rate of effectiveness when I am in my classroom. But I have also found that it has a 90 percent rate of effectiveness with younger siblings, and about an 80 percent rate of effectiveness with random children in a mall or grocery store. When I was little, I used to watch my mother stop children cold in their tracks with that look and I thought to myself that someday, *someday* I would inherit that gift. Well, the day has arrived and not a moment too soon. Now that this mini-friend has been subdued, I can continue my conference — the clock is a tickin'!

Why so concerned about the time you might ask? Well, if you haven't already gathered from the many context clues in the previous pages, Parent Teacher Conference night can be a bit of a zoo. Parents sitting up and down the hallways, loose children milling about unsupervised, all punctuated by rapid-fire conference time in which my Super Colleagues all nervously (and frequently) glance at the clock. Not because we are anxious for the night to be over (okay, well maybe we're a little anxious to go home…but really, conference night comes with the territory so most of us just suck it up), but anxious for the ominous moment when conferences officially end.

Maybe it's a mix of anxiety *and* humiliation. I say this because I know that I am mortified at 7:30 when the fire alarm goes off. Wait (insert pause for dramatic effect), let me repeat myself. I said, "WHEN THE FIRE ALARM GOES OFF."

That's right, in a stroke of genius (his words, not mine), The Visionary decided that the best way to end Parent Teacher Conference night was to set off a fire alarm and scare people out of the building. And possibly scare some grandparents into having a heart attack. You know, whatever.

I mean props to him for understanding that teachers want to get home, but really? A fire alarm? It's 7:29 exactly and I am finishing up with my last parent of the evening, desperately trying to wrap things up before the alarm sounds. As a result, I find myself glancing at the clock approximately every five seconds. I'm not sure if the parent knows what lies ahead, and am guessing that they assume that I either (a) suffer from a nervous tic, (b) moonlight as a stripper and am running late for work, or (c) I am totally disinterested in their concerns. As you can see, all their assumptions make me seem like a total jerk.

ME: "So I, uh (glance at clock) am very happy with uh (glance at clock) your child's progress. Um (glance at clock) I think you should continue everything you uh (glance at clock) do at home. I really um (glance at clock) appreciate your, uh, your…" (glance at clock… *damn, it's 7:30*)

Lights begin flashing as the alarms sounds in all its glory.

ME: (smiling awkwardly, I begin mouthing words in an overly exaggerated manner) "…your support! Thanks for coming in!"

PARENT: (clearly startled, also glancing around nervously, looking for signs of smoke, shouting) "WHAT'S GOING ON?"

ME: (also shouting) "CONFERENCES ARE OVER! WE
NEED TO LEAVE!"

We exchange an uncomfortable handshake as we
both grab our coats and dash for the door, hands over
our ears.

The Wheels on the Bus...

E'RE ALL ABOUT exposing our students to new experiences at our school. The Visionary loves to make speeches about all the things we expose our children to—chess, instrumental lessons, dance lessons, sports, art. But what really gets his motor running is field trips. The Visionary loves field trips. "Take them out of the building! Expose them to things," he proclaims.

As I giggled to myself (I mean, the guy is talking about "exposing" people for God sake!), I remembered the time that I exposed my little friends from the big city to rural farm life. My first year of teaching, everyone raved about this field trip to a nearby farm in Queens. And I thought to myself, "A farm in *Queens*?" but then let it go at that, because hey, what did I know, it was only my first year. So the trip gets scheduled and soon enough we're off to experience the joys of farming. I told my friends tales of cows, chickens, and pigs, basically whipping them into a farm-induced frenzy. As the bus pulled into the farm's parking lot (yes, this should have been my first indication that the farm was a load of crap: I mean, since when do farms have parking lots?), my friends' faces were glued to the windows, noses pressed to the glass feverishly searching the horizon for signs of animal life.

We trooped off the bus and were introduced to our Farm Tour Guide, who was a 20-something kid with a Mohawk (I know, I know, the signs were all over the place!). He led us to our first "farm adventure" (his words, not mine), which was a cow. A cow behind a fence. A cow behind a fence chained to a pole. A cow behind a fence chained to a pole with only about a four-foot range of movement. The cow, rendered essentially immobile, stood behind its fence, chained to the pole, and munched on the hay thrown at its feet. It might have been the saddest sight I have ever seen.

My friends, however, were undeterred. They were fascinated by this Farm Adventure and desperately tried to squeeze their little hands through the holes in the chain-link to poke at this poor, poor cow. Suddenly feeling as if I should join PETA, I asked our Farm Tour Guide if we could possibly move on to Adventure Number 2. Which we did. And all I can say is that it went downhill from there. The day ended with my friends visiting the "pumpkin patch." I use the term "pumpkin patch" loosely because where I come from, a dirty pile of pumpkins in the corner of a parking lot does not qualify as a patch. But, that's just me.

When we got back to school, I had my friends do some drawing and writing about what they had seen that day. Sadly, about 80 percent of them chose to draw the cow, complete with tiny little chain to connect it to its pole. I mean, can you imagine the looks they will get if they ever visit another farm in their lifetime, see the cow, and ask, "Where's its chain?"

And that is when I learned Field Trip Lesson #1: Don't trust a farm in Queens. Farms should be in legitimately farm-y places.

SINCE THAT FIRST "exposure" (seriously, that joke will never get old for me), field trips have remained an emotional roller coaster. For me, not for the kids. Every time my Super Colleagues and I plan one, it is almost guaranteed that some sort of mini-drama will ensue. And when The Weave schedules one for us? Well, then let the drama begin, because that trip is doomed from day one. Let's see, there was the time she scheduled a trip for a Saturday, and then got mad at us for pointing out her mistake before the permission slips went home. Then there was another time that she scheduled a trip on the same day that we had another trip, the time that she scheduled a trip for the same day we were performing in a whole-school assembly, and the time that she scheduled a trip but then didn't schedule any busses.

Perhaps my favorite was the time that she scheduled a trip for us three months in advance, but didn't tell me the trip was canceled until about ten minutes before we were supposed to go. We had our coats on and everything. We were about to walk out the door when…

…the phone rings.

ME: "We're learning!"

MS. WEAVALICIOUS: "Mrs. Mimi?"

ME: "Hi."

MS. WEAVALICIOUS: "Were you planning on going on the trip today?"

ME: "Um, yes."

MS. WEAVALICIOUS: "Because it was canceled. Didn't I tell you that?"

ME: "Um, no." (These are the moments when I think I should take more yoga classes to re-center myself because honestly, I just want to go postal on her right about now.)

MS. WEAVALICIOUS: "Yeah, they canceled on us last week. It must have slipped my mind. Sorry. But you'll work it out."

ME: "Um…so you've known for a week…"

MS. WEAVALICIOUS: "Don't you have anything else planned? I'm sure you can work something else out."

ME: "Um, no. I was planning on being gone from nine to one. I have things planned for the trip, not the classroom. Can I have coverage for just half an hour or something so I can pull something together?"

MS. WEAVALICIOUS: "Sorry. No. I'm sure you'll find a minute to pull something together. You'll work it out."

ME: "But all my kids are here, coats on, and ready to go. I need a moment to figure out what I'm going to do all day…"

MS. WEAVALICIOUS: "Just work it out."

ME: (You are lucky that we are surrounded by witnesses.) "Okay…well, I have two chaperones coming. I think they took the day off work. Can you call them and explain? I don't want them to come all the way back to school."

MS. WEAVALICIOUS: "Why can't you do it? I think you could work that out."

ME: (If she tells me to "work it out" one more time, I just might scream something I regret into the phone...) "Well, I can't do that because I'll be teaching and desperately scraping together a coherent day of instruction at the last minute."

MS. WEAVALICIOUS: "Don't you have a cell phone?"

ME: "Yes..."

MS. WEAVALICIOUS: "So you do it. You can work it out."

ME: "While I'm supposed to be teaching and lesson planning?"

MS. WEAVALICIOUS: "I'm sure you'll work it out."

Later, when I sent a child with an unrelated note to her office, they reported back that she was busy reading the paper.

Field Trip Lesson #2: Always have a backup plan.

AFTER THAT LITTLE "administrative snafu" (I'm trying to curse less in addition to Being More Positive in 2009), The Weave appointed one of our staff members to be a Field Trip Coordinator, so she could take that task off her plate. Which begs the question, can I hire someone to take some things off *my* plate?

I know, why do I even ask?

Anyway, I'm sure you are wondering what a Field Trip Coordinator even is. Hmmmm, where to start? Well, friends, a Field Trip Coordinator is someone very "special" who, despite being a "teacher," has endless amounts of free time all masked under the guise of Administrative Assistance periods. You say Administrative Assistance period, I say free time to shop online with your door's locked. Tomatoe, tomato.

I guess this person is otherwise known as an out-of-the-classroom-teacher-who-no-longer-needs-to-work-a-full-day-and-couldn't-teach-their-way-out-of-a-paper-bag-if-their-life-depended-on-it. Whew. Long title. Must be important. Glad we pay them a whole heck of a lot and they have tenure.

Shortly after one of my colleagues had been crowned Field Trip Coordinator, we were supposed to go on a trip that was initiated by Mr. Big White Guitar. Do I even need to finish the story? I think you can already tell that we did *not* go to the field trip if it was initiated and planned by this particular brain trust. Instead, we had a lovely adventure waiting outside in 32 degree weather for busses that were never ordered to show up. Then we sat in the lobby for 30 more minutes waiting for the Field Trip Coordinator to help us.

As we waited for the Field Trip Coordinator to help us and gradually began to have feeling return to our fingers, I was already expecting the worst and mentally pulling together a full day of instruction out of my, ahem, behind.

Enter the Field Trip Coordinator and Mr. Big White Guitar. They had supposedly been "problem solving" the situation together.

TFTC: "So, there aren't any busses."

ME: "No busses? Why not? I thought this trip was planned weeks ago?"

MR. BWG: "It was."

ME: "So where are the busses? Who was supposed to get them?"

TFTC: "He was." (pointing at Mr. BWG)

MR. BWG: "He was." (pointing at FTC)

ME: "Are you two serious?"

MR. BWG: "It's your fault, Field Trip Coordinator."

TFTC: "No, it's your fault, Mr. Big White Guitar."

MR. BWG: "No, yours."

TFTC: "Yours."

As you can read, the situation rapidly deteriorated.

And I just walked away with my class, popped in the emergency movie I keep in my classroom, and then went outside with my class to play in the snow.

All in all, we had a lovely day. I don't think the kids left feeling like they were cheated out of a fun experience. Actually, we had a pretty damn good time.

Thanks to me.

Field Trip Lesson #3: Always do things yourself.

JUST TO ADD a bit to my laundry list of complaints about field trips, let's spend a moment talking about chaperones, shall we? Just because the busses show up doesn't necessarily mean that it will be all smooth sailing from that point on. Now I am sure that many of you out there are amazing chaperones and are truly indispensable help to your child's teacher. To you parents, may I just say that you are welcome to come on any of my trips whenever you have the time, it doesn't matter that your child is not in my class. I have experienced your brand of wonderful and I would like some more, please.

Unfortunately, I have also come in contact with the other kind of chaperone, also known as the pain in my ass. After visiting the cow chained to a pole, I decided to take my friends to a genuine apple orchard. You know, to make up for their skewed idea of "the country" and all. To help monitor my 20 little ones as they ran loose in a field of trees, I brought along three parents. The first three parents that signed up, that is.

Big mistake.

We're at the apple orchard, and the Apple Orchard Man tells my group that each person is only allowed to pick two apples. The limit had to do with the fact that this was a working apple orchard and the owners had to make money off their crop, as well as the fact that other classes would be coming through and they wanted to leave some apples for them. Fine.

Fast-forward to the actual picking. My friends are running loose amongst the trees, lifting, twisting, and pulling apples off their branches. Their laughter fills the air and smiles are spread across their faces. It is right out of a movie. I am dutifully snapping pictures with my camera as to forever capture this moment when the Apple Orchard Man taps me on the shoulder.

APPLE MAN: "Um, miss?"

ME: "Yes?"

APPLE MAN: "Do you think you could speak to your chaperones?"

ME: "Is there a problem?"

APPLE MAN: "Well, I've seen two of them shove at least twenty apples each into their bag."

ME: "What?!"

APPLE MAN: "And they are encouraging your class to fill their pockets with extra apples. Some of them have four or five apples now."

ME: (mortified) "I'm so sorry. Of course. I will speak to them right away."

I walk away from Apple Man in search of my delinquent parents. I mean, really, people? We are on a field trip here! Trying to, oh, I don't know, set an example for young children? I spy an offender. Her bag is literally bursting with apple-shaped bulges.

ME: "Hi. Um, we have a bit of a problem. The Apple Man said that you had more than two apples."

PARENT: "No I don't."

ME: "Well, we can only take two apples...I guess you could pay for the extras...but really, we should only have two each."

PARENT: "I didn't take any apples."

ME: (sigh) "I can see leaves sticking out of your bag."

PARENT: "No you can't."

ME: (Are you kidding me?) "Look, I'm just passing the word. If you do happen to have more than two apples, could you please just take them out or pay for them? Thanks."

Field Trip Lesson #4: Carefully screen the parents who are going to come on field trips. And maybe run their fingerprints first...

TO BE TOTALLY fair (which I rarely am), I have to admit that there are times when I do love field trips. There was this one time that we went to the aquarium and just as we passed by the walrus exhibit, the walrus decided to swim up to the glass and give us a show. He waved his fins at my friends, blew bubbles...it was amazing. He stayed right near the glass for at least ten minutes. The entire time my friends, instead of screaming like I expected them to, stared mesmerized at the walrus, cooing phrases such as, "Hi, little walrus!" and "Will you high-five me again?" Then they turned around and looked at me, eyes all wide, and told me it was the "Best trip ever!" Um, I die. They were so cute and excited.

Of course, as we walked away a few friends caught the walrus taking a giant dump, also right near the glass. Hopefully, even fewer saw the walrus' friend swim up to begin (cough, cough) mating. It's like animals do that stuff on purpose in front of children.

Field Trip Lesson #5: Back away from the tank before the animal in question has the opportunity to poop. Or the animals start to do it.

I BOLSTERED MYSELF WITH fond memories of positive field trips past as our upcoming trip loomed on the horizon. Like the time my Super Colleagues and I all got matching T-shirts with the school mascot on the front and our names and room numbers on the back. Necessary? No. Fabulous? Yes.

In the effort to expose my friends to as much as possible, I try to maintain a Positive Attitude (my annual New Year's resolution since 2005), pull out my Mrs. Mimi T-shirt, and plan another one.

Yes, I know that field trips are physically and mentally exhausting. Yes, I know that the screaming on the bus has the potential to reach near-deafening levels. Yes, I know that everyone gets so excited that they can barely control themselves. And yes, I know there is never a man around to help with an entire group of boys who need to pee, which means I get to stand outside the bathroom and yell empty threats through the door jam until they come tumbling out, soaking wet, and leaving me to wonder exactly what they were up to in there. It means complaining (theirs, not mine...my complaining comes after the day is over and everyone goes home). And long lines. And other school groups who seem to be led by rude and obnoxious adults who encourage their class to push. Yes, yes, yes, I *know* all that...

Wait a minute...I lost my train of thought. Let's see. I like field trips...because...um, well...now that I think about it...hmmm. Exposure?

I love field trips because they always remind me of just how young and sweet my friends are. I love bringing them places and seeing them excited about learning. Not to get all after-school special on you, but I definitely get a thrill out of seeing my friends light up with a new discovery or when they look at me with those "I am having so much fun" eyes.

See? And you thought I couldn't come up with anything good.

So in the name of exposure and hope, I continue to plan field trips with my Super Colleagues. However, we have learned our lesson...or should I say lessons? Because there are many.

March was looming in the near future and is always the time of year when everyone is itching to get out of the building or have something to look forward to. In a rare proactive move we decided to plan a field trip. I say proactive, because we proactively planned a field trip rather than choosing to passively embrace the opportunity to complain about the endlessness that is March. Bravo to us: 2009 is full of Positive Attitudes!

But where to go? On that fateful day in Queens, we had learned our lesson and knew it was important to thoroughly check out the legitimacy of any given destination because it could easily be bullshit. Everyday my mailbox is stuffed with flyers for various potential field trips and half of them are total crap. Where could we go that was legit and fun for everyone? Hmmmm....

Well, we all love doing art with our little friends and taking them to a museum seemed like a perfect day in the making. Genius! We could take them to the Met! That place was definitely legit. I immediately began to fantasize about my friends and I picnicking in Central Park, then walking through the cherry blossoms to a nearby playground. After, we would bound up the stairs to the museum together and discover some fabulously inspirational piece of art. We would sprawl on the floor armed with pencils and erasers to do some sketching of our own. Sigh. It was the stuff of dreams. Or at least the stuff of teacher dreams.

The museum idea was perfect. And it came with a built-in backup plan, which as Field Trip Lesson #2 taught us, is absolutely necessary when many of the people you work with are basically morons. Morons with severe issues around calendaring. (There I go making up verbs again! What will be next?) If the museum fell through for any reason, we could spend the day in the park and use the city as our artistic inspiration. I could just bring around a good meaty artist read aloud and voilà! Backup plan.

As Field Trip Lesson #3 taught us, teachers must handle all the arrangements ourselves in order to avoid disaster. This was going to be a bit of a challenge for my Super Colleagues and me with our next step, which was making up and distributing the permission slips, because this particular task necessitated a photocopier. Now, as many of you who work in schools may already know, the photocopier is a hotbed of contention. I myself have spent a large amount of my time yelling at, crying over and dealing with the photocopier. Its permanent state seems to be (a) out of toner, (b) out of paper, or (c) jammed.

After many threats to take the photocopier out to the park with a baseball bat and go all Office Space on it, The Visionary decided that teachers were no longer allowed to touch the photocopier. Something about us being too smart or qualified to push all those buttons. Instead, some of the office staff would be making our copies, for which we were to fill out an official request. Not being smart enough to use the copier myself (which I find ironic considering that I am smart enough to teach people how to read), I put in a copy order, requesting 100 copies. The next morning, I found 100 copies in my mailbox. They were of the permission slip, all right; however, the copies were so jacked up that all of the most important information (how much the trip cost, the date, the times, the fact that kids need to bring a lunch...yeah, that stuff) had all been cut off. Evidently our office staff is not from the school of thought that believes in doing a test copy first. I had an internal debate: Would it be easier for me to just write the information 100 times at the bottom of each slip or should I attempt to put the permission slip in for copies again? As I reached for another copy request slip, I thought I could hear the rain forest screaming in quiet agony in the background and decided against putting the slip in for copies again. In the end, I did it myself, friends, I did it myself. Lesson learned.

After a solid week of hounding families to turn in the freaking permission slip already, I had 20 signed permission slips ready to go. But, oddly enough, I didn't have any parents volunteer to be a chaperone. Maybe it was the week of constant harassment (seriously, how hard is it to fill out a form completely?), or maybe it was the choice of venue that turned them off. Or maybe, just maybe, it was a sign that I shouldn't have any parent chaperones at all. Perhaps this was Field Trip Lesson #4 coming to life and reminding me that not every parent is helpful. Suddenly my mind was filled with visions of security guards chasing after my friends and our less-than-helpful parent volunteer who had leaned up against a valuable statue and sent it crashing to the ground. I shuddered and silently thanked the God of Classroom Teachers for reminding me of this poignant lesson. I would call one of my jobless friends for backup. Problem solved.

Excited about our upcoming adventure, and determined to make it a positive experience (*exposure?*), I spent many hours after school in my classroom stapling together makeshift sketchbooks for each of my friends to carry with them, suffering at least ten deep paper cuts. I organized everyone's name tags in case my worst nightmare came true and I actually lost a kid. I got the forms to get a subway pass for my entire class. I considered roping them to my body in the subway, and then decided to go with a more traditional buddy system. Dude, taking an entire class of kids in the subway and getting them all on and off the same car at the same time will never cease to set my pulse racing.

Then (finally!) the day of our trip was here. We were off! And, in spite of (or maybe because of) my hours of tedious preparation, we were having a fabulous time. Fabulous! The subway ride went without a hitch and only minimal hysterical screaming on my part. It was a gorgeous day. We had a very pleasant walk through Central Park and ran around in a local playground, a strategy I have found to be very useful in calming down a group of overexcited children before entering a quiet space such as a museum.

Then it was time for lunch. We found a beautiful clearing in the park and got ourselves set up in a wide circle. We sat down and opened up our lunches. Eating lunch out of the building is always very exciting for the kids. Almost all of them get free or reduced school lunch (read: "dog food and prison-grade meat") and so the experience of eating a lunch that their parents lovingly put together/ bought for them is a big freakin' deal. I know. I don't really get it, either. But it makes them happy.

Anyway, my friends were starting to eat and I frantically began running around twisting caps, opening bags, and inserting straws (those Capri Suns are no joke!). I then started to monitor what everyone had, preparing to enforce my Sandwich First law. I got to one of my friends and noticed that she was already eating her chips.

"Honey, you need to eat your sandwich first."

"I don't have one."

"Well, what else do you have?"

She showed me a bag of Doritos, a bag of Cheesy Poofs, and a big bottle of Blue Sugary Liquid masquerading as "juice."

She told me that is all her mother bought her. Her mom was in a hurry.

Hold on. I've been in a hurry, too, and have run into the store to buy lunch. But I grabbed a yogurt. Or a PB and J. My mom worked full time and raised me on her own, yet somehow I always managed to have a lunch that didn't come exclusively from the fats and oils sections of the food pyramid.

And it's not a money thing because those bags of chips are like $1.99 each...and if you have two bags, that's about $4. At the corner store closest to my school you can get a turkey sandwich and a bottle of water for $4.50. I know because that is what I brought on the trip.

I promptly gave my little friend half of my sandwich. I'm trying to cut back on carbs anyway.

Just like my earlier Field Trip Fantasy, we proudly marched up the stairs of the museum together. As we entered the museum, my previously boisterous friends fell silent. I like to think it was because they were blown away by the size of the museum or in awe of such a beautiful space, but really, I think they were just focused on holding their pee until we took our bathroom break.

On our way out of the bathroom and into the museum, we passed many other classes of students. As I watched the noisy, sometimes rude and out of control classes pass, I felt proud of my friends who stood quietly in line, respecting the other visitors around them just like I taught them to. It was going to be a good day. I could feel it.

I *love* doing art with my class. So I've been super antsy to go the museum with my friends. Like I told you, I have fantasized about my class spread out around me all inspired, busily sketching away in their little sketch pads...and here we were, sketching away in a room filled with amazing art! (sigh) It was beautiful.

I had sent away to the museum for educational materials and received an amazing map that detailed the various exhibits. Believe it or not, but The Weave is actually crazy supportive of our desire to teach art in our classrooms and has hooked us up with a good amount of really helpful professional development. With her help, my Super Colleagues and I had designed a pretty cool tour of various animal sculptures, statues, masks, and paintings. We were going to focus on the artists' use of lines to create the feeling of texture and movement in their work.

We gathered around a sculpture of a bold leopard, and I began to prompt my friends to think about the different kinds of lines they saw carved into the stone.

"I see straight lines for its teeth," noticed one friend.

"Beautiful," I encouraged, "what else do you see?"

"I see straight lines in its legs," said another friend.

"There are jagged lines to show the fur," offered a third.

"Nice work, guys! Anything else?" I ask.

"I see curved lines…" said a little voice from the back of the sculpture.

"What do the curved lines show?" I asked as I began to walk to the other side of the circle to see what my friend was talking about. If only I had known…I would have never asked.

"Um, I don't know," said my friend. She is pointing to the curved lines. I look.

And see that she is pointing directly at the leopard's, um, balls.

"Super! That's just great," I say quickly, anxious to move on before anyone questions me further as to exactly what part of the leopard my friend is talking about.

As we got up to move to our next destination, I began to see the entire museum in a whole new light. Suddenly, it was not the light-filled, quiet space with room after room of beautiful displays generally appreciated by art lovers. Rather, it was a world filled with boobs, balls, and butts generally appreciated by wide-eyed seven and eight year olds.

I looked at the map to see where we were headed. Gasp! We had to walk straight through the sculpture garden. I tried to quickly find an alternative route, but sadly, my directional skills are very poor and I was afraid I'd get us hopelessly lost. And so I made the game-time decision to stick to the plan and walk them through the sculpture garden, which to an eight year old, would appear to be a field of, well...

Penises. (Penii?? Hmm...I've never really considered the plural before...)

Yes, as we walked through the Greek and Roman statues, we passed beneath penis after glorious penis. Smooth bare behinds and perky bosoms completed the whole experience.

With one swift, expert Teacher Look (a.k.a. Look o'

Death) I silenced the wave of laughter that erupted from my line, forcing my class to walk through the World of European Penis silently. They all looked like their heads were going to explode.

Before our first official stop, we had a brief chat about how the human body is often considered to be a piece of art and aren't we proud of ourselves that we can appreciate that art like adults, without laughing?

They seemed to pick up what I was putting down.

The rest of the trip was fairly uneventful, although I couldn't help but notice the wide eyes, occasional snorts, and swallowed bursts of laughter as we continued our tour.

And, I'll be damned, when we made our way over to the African art exhibits, they got bigger.

I should have never forgotten about Lesson #5, "Back away from the tank before the animal in question has the opportunity to poop. Or do it. Or, I guess, show the parts needed to do it." I never imagined that this lesson could come into play, in a strangely literal way, at an art museum.

Huh.

Somewhere a Fat Lady Is Singing

IT IS JUNE. I can't believe it is already here. June is a very strange time in schools. On one hand, you are pumped that summer is coming. After all, having summers off is one of the big perks of being a teacher. And while it is not the reason we become teachers, it is pretty sweet. But on the other hand, another year is over and that is kind of sad. I feel like I've worked so hard with and on my little friends all year, and now some of them will move on to new teachers, and some of them will move to another school, and I'll never see them again. Yet, while I am on my own personal emotional roller coaster, I also have about ten million things to do: clean out my classroom to be packed up for the summer, fill out report cards, have final meetings with some parents, begin thinking about *next* year, and deal with the mountain of paperwork that goes along with permanent files and sending children to their next teacher. On top of all that (yes, there's more), we have insane amounts of end-of-the-year activities, like Field Day, class picnics, and awards assemblies.

I have observed that teachers deal with this end-of-the-year-palooza in many different ways. Some simply stop teaching. Instead, they let the kids read and play games while they set about checking things off their lists. And it's not just the usual lazy suspects such as The Fanny Pack who engage in this sort of behavior. I am always amazed with how many teachers think it is easier to just do whatever they want and stay out of trouble while the teacher attends to cleaning and paperwork.

Other teachers turn their classrooms into a Fun Fest and do nothing but show movies, go outside to play, and have parties. Sadly, many of these teachers also forget about or ignore the million other things they should be doing and end up in an almost catatonic state during the last week of school when they have to power through everything.

I try to aim for the middle. I want to use the month of June to, I don't know, *teach*, but I also want it to feel like a fun ending to our time together. So we celebrate and do fun things like make scrapbooks of our year, but we also get a lot of reading, writing, and 'rithmatic done, too. I am nothing without my routine.

To cope, I am in full-blown listing mode. I have so many lists that I have to create a master list of all my lists just to keep track of them all. I know, it's a sickness. But it is also a thing of beauty. I have color coded (by day, of course) everything that I need to get done before the last day of school in an effort to avoid my usual End-of-the-Year Panic.

Let the chaos begin!

*U*ESTERDAY WAS FIELD DAY! Another day that signals the end of the year. In years past, Field Day was quite literal, meaning we literally sat in a field all day. No games, no relay races, no nothing. You told your class to BYO towel and maybe some outdoor games or toys and then we would go to the nearby public park and sit. That's it. Perhaps a teacher or two would get up and throw the occasional Frisbee or organize a game of tag, but aside from that the scene would simply consist of approximately eight classes worth of children and their teachers lying in the park all day. Excuse me, I mean, lying in the *field* all day...hence Field Day.

But this year was different. Someone motivated, I'm not sure exactly who, organized (wait for it...are you sitting?) a schedule that made sense! Whoo hoo! We can automatically eliminate The Weave, The Fanny Pack, and The Bacon Hunter from the list of possible suspects. It must have been another teacher. Only another teacher could pull off the organizational thing of beauty that was this year's Field Day.

Every grade wore a different color and each class represented a different country. Clearly modeled after the Olympics, we had an opening ceremony where we talked about sportsmanship and cheered for the other teams. It was wonderful. The kids were pumped and we had a day full of relay races, hula hoops, obstacle courses, and sprinklers ahead of us. I can't tell you how nice it was to relax and let my kids just be kids rather than hard-core students. They are so much cuter that way!

My class began the day with parachute games, a beach-ball relay race, and potato sack races. I took some of the funniest pictures I have ever taken! Kids with smiles so big you might think their faces were going to crack. And one thing that made me so proud (and so sad to let them go next year) was watching my friends cheer for one another, congratulate one another, and work together as a team. And when we lost, which was a rare occasion because we seriously *rocked it* all day (thought the teacher who secretly gloated to all the other teachers but heard herself say out loud to her students, "winning is not important, friends"), I saw so many of my kids turn to the winners and congratulate them or tell each other that they tried their best and had fun. I know, sounds a little too Hallmarky and perfect, but these moments can be few and far between so I like to play them up and milk them for all their worth when they actually happen. So please allow me a little schmaltz.

We took a much-needed break for lunch, where I literally ran up the stairs to the bathroom. It takes a lot to get me to run (or wear shorts, and I did that, too), but today was no joke. I felt like my event for the day was the Holding My Pee Relay in which teachers acted like they didn't want to dash inside but when the bell rang for lunch we all streaked (not naked, you dirty birds) to the bathroom, and rather than passing a baton, worked together to pass off our lone two stalls as quickly as possible. And to the teachers who participated yesterday, I say "Good job…great teamwork!"

After lunch it was our turn to play in the sprinklers. Yes, I said sprinklers. We have a small play yard (in addition to the larger play yard) with fun equipment for the kids to climb on and these ridiculously cool sprinklers that go very unused for most of the year. It's this huge area that is set down in the ground and away from the monkey bars with three huge fountains that spray up out of the ground. We so did not have *that* when I was little (sigh). Anywho, if you throw down some serious rules about wearing your bathing suit to school and keeping it on until you dry, it can be superfun.

I took more pictures of everyone laughing, screaming, and running through the water. They were freaking adorable! (Please prepare yourself for another shmaltzy moment.) No one was pushing, no one got left out, and everyone was having fun. They were acting like sweet little seven and eight year olds on that fabulous day when the teacher let them play in the sprinklers. It was awesome. They started a game where they dared each other to see how long they could stand over one of the fountains in the cold water. So cute! One kid would go in the middle over a fountain and stand there, screaming and dancing around, while the rest of the group counted how many seconds they could stand it. It was like keg stands for seven year olds. (Remember the good old days filled with keg stands...where your evening consisted of your friends holding you upside down as you sucked on a tap handle and everyone around you cheered and counted? Ah, memories...)

Wait...what was I talking about? Beer? That can't be right...oh yes, sprinklers and Field Day, and my sweet little friends.

So I saunter over to the woman in charge of the sprinklers for the day. For my first few years at this school, I thought she was the gardener, because I only saw her in the fall and spring—never winter—and every time I saw her, she was working in the small patch of garden that we have outside the school. I just assumed we hired someone from the community to plant stuff. Then, three years into my teaching, I find out that she is a *counselor* who is supposed to work with *children* and not plants. Go figure. So, from now on, we shall call her The Gardener.

Now keep in mind that I have spoken to this woman probably two other times in the *seven years* I have been working at this school. We smile in the hall and all that other crap, but we rarely actually speak. So I walk over to her ready to make some polite small talk as my friends frolic. I mean wouldn't it just be awkward to have two adults in a small space who just stood there and didn't even attempt to have some small talk? You would think so…but that doesn't even compare to the awkwardness that I experienced as a result of my foolish attempt to be polite.

ME: "Aren't they cute? It must be so much fun to be out here today and see all the kids running through the sprinklers. It's nice to see them act like little kids, isn't it?"

THE GARDENER: "Um yes. Are those your children playing the sprinklers like that? Standing over the fountain for several seconds at a time?"

ME: "Yes." (Proud that my students are behaving so nicely
and have created this game where everyone plays and
cheers for each other...sigh...I love this class. And I
swear to you, it is all *fun* and *innocent* until...)

THE GARDENER: "Well you need to get them to stop. We
don't need children standing there having orgasms.
The next thing you know they will all be shivering
and shaking and oooooohhhhhhhhh."

ME: Did she just say what I thought she said? Is this really
what our *third conversation ever* is going to be about?
I wonder how she even got the balls to say this to me
when I doubt that she even knows my name...what
do I say...what do I say...ummmmmm) "Oh. I, uh,
think it's, um, fine. I'm...I'm going to go, uh, stand
over here now."

Yes, that is what I came up with, folks. And I did.
I did go stand over there, away from The Gardener and
her weird sexual fantasies about sprinklers.

What a way to wrap up the year with my co-workers!
Perhaps for the remainder of the year, I will try to stay
in my classroom and continue making lists.

I HAD JUST DISMISSED my friends and was on the computer, considering the possibility of *typing* my lists (my mastery of procrastination is awe-inspiring) when I received a fairly obnoxious email that reeked of I'm-going-to-pretend-that-I-actually-do-something from our favorite staff developer, The Bacon Hunter. (Or is she really in charge of ordering everyone breakfast in the morning? This is the source of many heated lunchtime debates among teachers...). This lovely and thoughtful email detailed the process by which the teachers are to return *all* of their math supplies exactly 11 full school days before the last day (God forbid that she put in a full day or — gasp — stayed late to do her job!). Before our math supplies are officially returned to her, the contents of our boxes must be checked to ensure that nothing is missing. This is ridiculous for several reasons:

1. Aren't we supposed to be (dare I say it?) teaching until the last day of school?

2. It assumes that I intend to walk off with pockets full of Base 10 blocks. Really? As if I'm preparing for an impending place value emergency? Well, maybe my sister will totally flip at the grocery store over the cost of meat for our summer BBQ and I'll need to whip out some flats and longs so that we can divide

the burden into equal shares… hmmm, I guess that could happen. Regardless, I'm totally not going to steal any cubes.

Oooo…wait a minute. Mr. Mimi always says I make the mistake of assuming that everyone is a teacher and understands "the teacher talk." For those of you not lucky enough to spend your day with children, Base 10 blocks are tools we use to teach basic place value to children (you know, the hundreds place, tens place, and ones place?). Okay, now go back and re-read number 2…we're pausing…and you're laughing. Onto number 3!

3. It's amazing to me that so many people who have no direct contact with children get to order me around as if *I'm* the low man on the totem pole. When did teachers get to be the *least* important people in schools?

4. Did I mention that this particular staff developer totally *sucks*?

However, because I *rock* and always do what I'm told (thanks, Mom!), I load up my oh-so-handy overhead projector cart with massive piles of mathematics manuals, manipulatives, and more. In my typical anal-retentive fashion, I check off each of the items on my perfectly crisp and freshly printed checklist and head for the elevator. When I arrive at the unofficial breakfast lounge (excuse me) I mean…when I arrive at the staff developers' office, I become a part of the following scene:

ME: "Hey, where would you like all this math stuff?"

HER: (while totally slumped over her desk, seriously, cheek in *full contact* with the desk.) "What?"

ME: "I brought up most of the math supplies you asked for. Today is the half day and I had time to do it so I thought I would get it out of the way."

HER: (insert sound of teeth sucking) "Well they can't come in here."

ME: "Wait, so the supplies *you* requested be returned to *you* in a timely manner can't be put in *your* office?"

HER: "No."

ME: "Well, they are not going back in my classroom now that I've already packed them all up. Where do you suggest they go? Hey, could you pick your head up off your desk or something?"

HER: (more teeth sucking) "They can go in the closet."

Me: "On the second floor? Across the hall from my room where I came from?" (internal monologue: I hate you I hate you I hate you…PICK YOUR HEAD UP!)

HER: "Yeah." (Head returns to original position, slumped over; maybe there's bacon hiding somewhere on the desk and tempting her?)

ME: (huge sigh) "Okay, is it unlocked?" (internal monologue: I hate you I hate you I hate you...get up get up
GET UP! If there is bacon there, it's cold by now!)

HER: "I'm not going in there without a mask or something. It's nasty."

ME: "Um, yes, but is it unlocked because I have other
things to do...." (OH MY GOD...DO SOMETHING!)

Okay...I'll stop there because the scene then deteriorates into more teeth sucking and bacon hunting. I
give up and push my cart full of mathematical fun back
down the hall to the elevator. And no, the closet was *not*
unlocked when I got there. In fact it was very locked.
Figures.

So, in my final act of passive aggression toward this
woman, I left my math supplies in a huge heap outside
the door with a huge note that read:

Bacon Hunter,

Here are the supplies you requested. Thanks for
volunteering to put them away in the closet.

Mrs. Mimi

I then returned to my classroom, checked "return
math supplies" off my list, and began to work on filling
out report cards.

$\mathcal{L}$AST NIGHT, BEFORE leaving school, I placed my carefully completed report cards in a folder on the table in the front of my room. Don't be fooled, completing report cards is no small feat. First, I must convince myself that someone is actually going to look at them and give them thoughtful pause. Then, I must convince myself that despite the fact that the report cards aren't actually aligned with anything we do during the year, that they can somehow be manipulated to accurately reflect each child's progress. And lastly, after 30 minutes of relentless bubbling (yes, they are scan tron) I must convince myself to not give in to the temptation to just make up a little pattern and bubble at will. You know, a little 1, 2, 1, 2, 1, 2, 3, 1, 2, 1, 2, 1, 2, 3. (In case you're wondering, we no longer give the traditional A, B, C, D, and F letter grades. Someone downtown was "thinking outside the box" and revolutionized teaching by switching those little letters to numbers. Groundbreaking, I know.)

So I do the report cards. And then I relish picking up a new, blue Sharpie and boldly crossing "report cards" off my colossal To Do list. As I have said, at this point in the year my To Do list has birthed little baby To Do lists and it feels like everything is spiraling out of control. So you can imagine my nerdy-nerds-a-lot satisfaction. Ah, I can almost smell the Sharpie now...

Anyway, I put the report cards on the table, lock my door, and skip home.

Okay. I didn't skip. But I did have a smile on my face as I carefully stepped over the chicken bones and made my way to the bus.

Fast-forward to the next morning. I drag myself out of bed (not so smiley) and get my behind to work. I open the door to my room and...

...all the chairs in the front of the classroom are knocked over...

...there are huge black boot prints on the desks...and...

NO REPORT CARDS.

They are gone.

But, in my Zen state of calm that only comes when your professional life is in such utter disarray that you internally just give up, I decide not to panic and ask around. After being repeatedly told that "I don't know, but you should ask so-and-so," I begin to realize that they might truly be gone (a.k.a. someone stole them or threw them out). I can't quite wrap my head around why anyone would want to steal scan tron report cards, so I now believe that they have been thrown out.

I go downstairs to talk to our custodian. (Have I mentioned that I have a billion other things to do? Yes? No? Well, I do...and those things do *not* include solving the Great Report Card Mystery.) The custodian tells me that she didn't sweep my room or vacuum yesterday (sweet, right?), but she did take away my trash and no, she did not throw anything out. She also is unable to explain the big, black boot prints on the desks.

I may sound calm now, but at the time, I was literally seething. Who are these boot-clad circus monkeys dancing around my room and stealing report cards?

And now, I will explain how this situation did a complete 180 and why I think that now, I might *be* one of the circus monkeys...

I told one of my colleagues what happened and she said, "Are you going to have to do them again?"

And I thought, "Um, hell no!"

I went to the computer guy (who scans the scan tron) and he said, "No problem, we'll just print you out some more."

Just like that. "No problem, we'll just print you out some more." Like I was some kind of circus monkey that would nod my head, scratch my pits, dutifully grab a pencil, and get ready to bubble.

But why wouldn't he think that? I get told to do all kinds of crap without any reason or purpose. And the saddest thing is, I *do it*. Out of guilt, out of obligation, out of responsibility, and out of a perverse need to prove to everyone that I can do it all (dammit) and better than anyone else. (Are you secretly thinking that I deserved to get my report cards stolen?)

So there it is. I am one of the circus monkeys who has officially been screwed by a fellow circus monkey.

ODAY WAS THE last day of school. It wasn't easy, though. The kids were pumped, and I was ready to be done, but we had to endure another useless half day in which no learning took place at all. Add to that the lack of structure that permeates the school on the last day, combine that with some doughnut holes, and you have a recipe for a super headache. I was sad to see many of them go (actually teared up a bit), but there's something about that last day and all the chaos surrounding putting one's classroom to bed that makes it much easier to say good-bye (and don't let the door hit you on the...).

I don't expect many gifts. My students can't afford them, but occasionally families get creative. Some of you may remember my heartwarming tale in which I received an actual G-string from a student. However, I did get some very sweet cards this year, and a few overly shiny necklaces lovingly selected from the Dollar Store. All very thoughtful. And then...

I had a parent (who I really like) come up to me with a real winner.

PARENT: "Here you go, Mrs. Mimi. I know you can use this!" (She hands me a brown paper bag) "Sorry I didn't get a chance to wrap it."

ME: "Don't worry. You didn't have to do this. Thank you so much for thinking of me."

I take the bag and peek inside to find...a bottle of Malibu rum.

Yes, booze.

Now, I do happen to enjoy the fruity cocktail topped off with a bit of alcoholic coconut-flavored love, but...we are in a school. And I work inside that school. I do *not* sit outside the school sipping on a little gin and juice. Or at least, I don't yet.

I thank the parent (isn't it the thought that counts?)

and quickly fold over the top of the bag, trying desperately to hide the fact that now I am leading my class upstairs holding a bottle of booze.

Fast-forward to that night. I am home from work and officially on vacation. I'm slightly drunk. No, no, not off the Malibu. But I did go have one or two (or five) beers with the girls to celebrate the end of the year.

Mr. Mimi comes home and congratulates me on finishing the year in one piece. I tell him to reach into my bag to see the thoughtful gift that I had received. I am literally dying for him to see it…I mean, it's just too good.

He pulls out the bottle of Malibu. "Get out!" he shouts, "A *parent* gave you this? Which one?"

As I begin to tell him the story, he holds up the bottle to the light (why do people do that?) and interrupts me, saying,

"This bottle is open."

"What?"

"It's open. Did you have any?"

"Uh, no."

"So they gave you an open bottle of rum? And look, there's some missing."

He holds up the bottle again, and we notice that it isn't full. Someone has definitely taken a sip or two (or five).

Hmmmmm....

MMMM, COCKTAIL. As I take my first sip of the fruity umbrella-topped love that is my cocktail, I am interrupted by a young man who has sidled up to the bar to chat me up while, alas, my colleagues are in the bathroom. The bar is dark, smelly, sticky. Not the type of place that you go to meet new people...or at least, not where I go to meet new people. Where you go to meet new people is your own business, I suppose. However, the dank, dark atmosphere and "leave us alone" attitude is exactly why we went to this bar on the last day of school.

Guy at the Bar looks at me, and I can see him trying to decide what his opening line is going to be. I am alone in the corner of the bar, with no way to get out.

Crap, crap, crap. He is breaking focus from my cocktail!

And honestly? I am hanging out with my Super Colleagues and don't really want any new friends. Today (or really any day), it is nearly impossible for me to talk about anything but school. And myself. Really, myself in school. And my kids. That's it. That is the extent of my conversation and I like it that way. My husband says that when the school girls all get together, we just sit there and shout stories at one another, all interruptions and trying to one up each other with increasingly tragic tales of overworked, underpaid, woe. He thinks it's hysterical (or highly annoying) to watch us all try to outdo each other, screaming over cocktails and pausing only to take sips or cry hysterically with laughter.

He calls it a screaming match. I call it therapy.

And really, tonight I only want to talk to my teacher friends. So, in this moment, I begin to consider how I can get out of talking to this guy. Do I flash him my wedding ring? That's a bit presumptuous, isn't it? I mean, I'm not *that* pretty. Do I let out an obnoxious, unattractive, and off-putting belch? (Because I can and I will.) No, maybe he likes that sort of thing. I am in a dirty bar after all.

GUY AT THE BAR: "So what do you do?"

ME: (Okay…get out of this quick…what to do…what to do.) "I'm a teacher." (Nice save, loser.)

GUY AT THE BAR: (big smile, a little too big, like he has a weird teacher fantasy involving half-glasses and a yardstick) "Oh, that's so cute!"

Cute? And that's when I decided how to get out of it. Oh, it's on...

I will spare you the rage. Because, really? I just want you to smile, nod, and tell me I'm fabulous.

Acknowledgments

So MANY PEEPS, so little time. I thought maybe I would begin by thanking the fine people at Sharpie for all those lovely little moments alone with a brand new pen and my lists. You have no idea how responsible you are for my sanity.

To all my readers—you are rockstars! When I started this blog, I never imagined that anyone would read it, much less find me funny! Your comments and emails have meant so much to me. I hope this book does you proud!

Truly, I would like to thank Kaplan Publishing for reaching deep into the blogosphere and helping me bring Mrs. Mimi's voice to a larger audience. It means a lot that you could see past all my complaining, jokes and stories of urine to find a person struggling to be a better teacher. Also, a huge thank you to Brendan Deneen, agent and friend du jour. If you thought you had gotten rid of me after years of tennis camp and summer theatre, you thought wrong, friend, you thought wrong.

A very special thanks to the UConn eMBA Study Group #4. I think the blog was all your idea in the first place! Thanks for being such avid readers, especially when you should have been paying attention in class. Your laughter, support and feedback were, and still are, fabulous.

Cricket, Aimee and Aaron…you have always been Mrs. Mimi's biggest fans. Thank you for reading, thank you for encouraging me, thank you for thinking I'm funny and thank you for all the BLTs.

To my family…Mom, Fred, Nathan, Karen, Dale, Eric and Marie…what can I say? Thanks for putting up with me? Thanks for all the cheese? Your support (read: constant tolerance of me when I think I'm funny) is amazing. I can't imagine eight funnier people. Seriously, we're hilarious. I love you.

Nathan (a.k.a. Mr. Mimi), thank you for talking me in off the ledge when I thought the mice were going to eat my shoes. (True story.) Thank you for listening when I came home from work and couldn't talk about anything else. Thank you for understanding how much teaching means to me. Thank you for all the encouragement, love and laughter a wife could ever imagine.

And to the real Mimi, my thoroughly overfed and wonderful cat…it's dry food time!

About the Author

MRS. MIMI IS Jennifer Scoggin, a second grade teacher at a public elementary school in New York City, where she has taught both first and second grades for the past eight years. She graduated from Connecticut College in 2000, where she completed her teacher certification program with a degree in Human Development. Mrs. Mimi also holds a Master's degree from Columbia University's Teachers College in sociology and education, with a focus on educational policy. Currently, Mrs. Mimi is a sixth-year doctoral student in the Curriculum and Instruction department at Teachers College.